YOUR P...
HORO...
2015

AQUARIUS

YOUR PERSONAL HOROSCOPE 2015

AQUARIUS

21st January–19th February

igloobooks

igloobooks

Published in 2014
by Igloo Books Ltd

Cottage Farm
Sywell
NN6 0BJ
www.igloobooks.com

Produced for Igloo Books by W. Foulsham & Co. Ltd, The Old Barrel Store,
Drayman's Lane, Marlow, Bucks SL7 2FF, England

HUN001 0714
2 4 6 8 10 9 7 5 3 1
ISBN: 978-1-783-43636-1

This is an abridged version of material originally published
in Old Moore's Horoscope and Astral Diary.

Printed and manufactured in China

CONTENTS

CONTENTS

INTRODUCTION

Your Personal Horoscopes have been specifically created to allow you to get the most from astrological patterns and the way they have a bearing on not only your zodiac sign, but nuances within it. Using the diary section of the book you can read about the influences and possibilities of each and every day of the year. It will be possible for you to see when you are likely to be cheerful and happy or those times when your nature is in retreat and you will be more circumspect. The diary will help to give you a feel for the specific 'cycles' of astrology and the way they can subtly change your day-to-day life. For example, when you see the sign ☿, this means that the planet Mercury is retrograde at that time. Retrograde means it appears to be running backwards through the zodiac. Such a happening has a significant effect on communication skills, but this is only one small aspect of how the Personal Horoscope can help you.

With Your Personal Horoscope the story doesn't end with the diary pages. It includes simple ways for you to work out the zodiac sign the Moon occupied at the time of your birth, and what this means for your personality. In addition, if you know the time of day you were born, it is possible to discover your Ascendant, yet another important guide to your personal make-up and potential.

Many readers are interested in relationships and in knowing how well they get on with people of other astrological signs. You might also be interested in the way you appear to very different sorts of individuals. If you are such a person, the section on Venus will be of particular interest. Despite the rapidly changing position of this planet, you can work out your Venus sign, and learn what bearing it will have on your life.

Using Your Personal Horoscope you can travel on one of the most fascinating and rewarding journeys that anyone can take – the journey to a better realisation of self.

THE ESSENCE OF AQUARIUS

Exploring the Personality of Aquarius the Water Carrier

(21ST JANUARY – 19TH FEBRUARY)

What's in a sign?

Oh, what a wonderful person you can be! Despite a number of contradictions and one of the most complicated natures to be found anywhere in the zodiac, you certainly know how to make friends and influence people. Your ruling planet is Uranus, one of the more recently discovered members of the solar system's family. It rules modern communications, such as radio and television, and also has a response to the recent discoveries of science. It is within the world of 'the modern' that you reside and you have little or no difficulty keeping up with the ever-increasing pace of life.

People naturally like you and it's not surprising. You are open, liberal, and rarely judgmental, and you are often surrounded by deeply original and even eccentric types. Life to you is a storybook full of fascinating tales. Aquarians amass information 'on the hoof' and very little passes you by. Understanding what makes others tick is meat and drink to you and proves to be a source of endless joy. Unlike the other Air signs of Gemini and Libra, you are able to spend long hours on your own if necessary and always keep your mind active.

Aquarians have great creative potential; they are refined, often extremely well educated and they remain totally classless. This makes it easy for you to get on with just about any sort of person and also explains your general success in the material world. You are fascinating, original, thought-provoking and even quite deep on occasions. Matters that take months for others to synthesise, you can absorb in minutes. It is clear to everyone that you are one of life's natural leaders, but when you head any organisation you do so by co-operation and example because you are not in the least authoritarian.

In love you can be ardent and sincere – for a while at least. You need to be loved and it's true that deeply personal relationships can be a problem to you if they are not supplying what is most important to you. Few people know the real you, because your nature exists on so many different levels. For this reason alone you defy analysis and tend to remain outside the scope of orthodoxy. And because people can't weigh you up adequately, you appear to be more fascinating than ever.

Aquarius resources

Your chief resource has to be originality. Like a precious Fabergé Egg you are a single creation, unique and quite unlike anything else to be found anywhere in the world. Of course, used wrongly, this can make you seem odd or even downright peculiar. But Aquarians usually have a knack for creating the best possible impression. The chances are that you dress in your own way and speak the words that occur to you, and that you have a side to your nature that shuns convention. Despite this you know how to adapt when necessary. As a result your dinner parties would sport guests of a wide variety of types and stations. All of these people think they know the 'real you' and remain committed to helping you as much as they can.

The natural adaptability that goes along with being an Aquarian makes it possible for you to turn your hand to many different projects. And because you are from an Air sign, you can undertake a variety of tasks at the same time. This makes for a busy life, but being on the go is vital for you and you only tire when you are forced into jobs that you find demeaning, pointless or downright dull.

All of the above combines to make a nature that has 'resourcefulness' as its middle name. Arriving at a given set of circumstances – say a specific task that has to be undertaken – you first analyse what is required. Having done so you get cracking and invariably manage to impress all manner of people with your dexterity, attention to detail and downright intelligence. You can turn work into a social event, or derive financial gain from your social life. Activity is the keyword and you don't really differentiate between the various components of life as many people would.

Success depends on a number of different factors. You need to be doing things you enjoy as much you can and you simply cannot be held back or bound to follow rules that appear to make no sense to you. You respond well to kindness, and generally receive it because you are so considerate yourself. But perhaps your greatest skill of all is your ability to make a silk purse out of a sow's ear. You are never stuck for an idea and rarely let financial restrictions get in your way.

Beneath the surface

'What you see is what you get' could never really be considered a sensible or accurate statement when applied to the sign of Aquarius. It's difficult enough for you to know the way your complicated mind works, and almost impossible for others to sort out the tangle of possibilities. Your mind can be as untidy as a tatty workbox on occasions and yet at other times you can see through situations with a clarity that would dazzle almost any observer. It really depends on a whole host of circumstances, some of which are inevitably beyond your own control. You are at your best when you are allowed to take charge from the very start of any project, because then your originality of thought comes into play. Your sort of logic is unique to you, so don't expect anyone else to go down the same mental routes that you find easy to follow.

Aquarians are naturally kind and don't tend to discriminate. This is not a considered matter, it's simply the way you are. As a result it is very hard for you to understand prejudice, or individuals who show any form of intolerance. The fairness that you exemplify isn't something that you have to work at – it comes as naturally to you as breathing does.

You can be very peculiar and even a little cranky on occasions. These aspects of your nature are unlikely to have any bearing on your overall popularity, but they do betray a rather unusual mindset that isn't like that of any other zodiac sign. When you feel stressed you tend to withdraw into yourself, which is not really good for you. A much better strategy would be to verbalise what you are thinking, even though this is not always particularly easy to do.

There are many people in the world who think they know you well, but each and every one of them knows only one Aquarian. There are always more, each a unique individual and probably as much of a mystery to you as they would be to all your relatives and friends, that is if any of them suspected just how deep and mysterious you can be. Despite these facts, your mind is clear and concise, enabling you to get to the truth of any given situation almost immediately. You should never doubt your intuitive foresight and, in the main, must always back your hunches. It is rare indeed for you to be totally wrong about the outcome of any potential situation and your genuine originality of thought is the greatest gift providence has bestowed on you.

Making the best of yourself

Interacting with the world is most important to you. Although you can sometimes be a good deal quieter than the other Air signs of Gemini and Libra, you are still a born communicator, with a great need to live your life to the full. If you feel hemmed in or constrained by circumstances, you are not going to show your best face to family, friends or colleagues. That's why you must move heaven and earth to make certain that you are not tied down in any way. Maintaining a sense of freedom is really just a mental state to Aquarius but it is absolutely vital to your well-being.

As far as work is concerned you need to be doing something that allows you the room you need to move. Any occupation that means thinking on your feet would probably suit you fine. All the same you feel more comfortable in administrative surroundings, rather than getting your hands dirty. Any profession that brings change and variety on a daily basis would be best. You are a good team operator, and yet can easily lead from the front. Don't be frightened to show colleagues that you have an original way of looking at life and that you are an inveterate problem solver.

In terms of friendship you tend to be quite catholic in your choice of pals. Making the best of yourself means keeping things that way. You are not naturally jealous yourself but you do tend to attract friends who are. Make it plain that you can't tie yourself down to any one association, no matter how old or close it may be. At least if you do this nobody can suggest that they weren't warned when you wander off to talk to someone else. Personal relationships are a different matter, though it's hardly likely that you would live in the pocket of your partner. In any situation you need space to breathe, and this includes romantic attachments. People who know you well will not try to hem you in.

Don't be frightened to show your unconventional, even wild side to the world at large. You are a bold character, with a great deal to say and a natural warmth that could melt an iceberg. This is the way providence made you and it is only right to use your gifts to the full.

The impressions you give

You are not a naturally secretive person and don't hold back very much when it comes to speaking your mind. It might be suggested therefore that the external and internal Aquarian is more or less the same person. Although generally true, it has to be remembered that you have a multi-faceted nature and one that adapts quickly to changing circumstances. It is this very adaptability that sets you apart in the eyes of the world.

You often make decisions based on intuitive foresight and although many Aquarians are of above average intelligence, you won't always make use of a deep knowledge of any given situation. In essence you often do what seems right, though you tend to act whilst others are still standing around and thinking. This makes you good to have around in a crisis and convinces many of those looking on that you are incredibly capable, relaxed and confident. Of course this isn't always the case, but even a nervous interior tends to breed outward action in the case of your zodiac sign, so the world can be forgiven for jumping to the wrong conclusion.

People like you – there's no doubt about that. However, you must realise that you have a very upfront attitude, which on occasions is going to get you into trouble. Your occasional weirdness, rather than being a turn-off, is likely to stimulate the interest that the world has in you. Those with whom you come into contract invariably find your personality to be attractive, generous, high-spirited and refreshing. For all these reasons it is very unlikely that you would actually make many enemies, even if some folk are clearly jealous of the easy way you have with the world.

One of the great things about Aquarians is that they love to join in. As a result you may find yourself doing all sorts of things that others would find either difficult or frightening. You can be zany, wild and even mad on occasions, but these tendencies will only get you liked all the more. The world will only tire of you if you allow yourself to get down in the dumps or grumpy – a very rare state for Aquarius.

The way forward

In terms of living your life to the full it is probable that you don't need any real advice from an astrologer. Your confidence allows you to go places that would make some people shiver, whilst your intuitive foresight gives you the armoury you need to deal with a world that can sometimes seem threatening. Yet for all this you are not immune to mental turmoil on occasions, and probably spend rather too much time in the fast lane. It's good to rest, a fact that you need to remember the next time you find yourself surrounded by twenty-seven jobs, all of which you are trying to undertake at the same time.

The more the world turns in the direction of information technology, the happier you are likely to become. If others have difficulty in this age of computers, it's likely that you relish the challenges and the opportunities that these artificial intelligences offer. You are happy with New Age concepts and tend to look at the world with compassion and understanding. Despite the fact that you are always on the go, it's rare for you to be moving forward so fast that you forget either the planet that brought you to birth, or the many underprivileged people who inhabit parts of it. You have a highly developed conscience and tend to work for the good of humanity whenever you can.

You might not be constructed of the highest moral fibre known to humanity, a fact that sometimes shows when it comes to romantic attachments. Many Aquarians play the field at some time in their lives and it's certain that you need a personal relationship that keeps you mentally stimulated. Although your exterior can sometimes seem superficial, you have a deep and sensitive soul – so perhaps you should marry a poet, or at least someone who can cope with the twists and turns of the Aquarian mind. Aquarians who tie themselves down too early, or to the wrong sort of individual, invariable end up regretting the fact.

You can be deeply creative and need to live in clean and cheerful surroundings. Though not exactly a minimalist you don't like clutter and constantly need to spring-clean your home – and your mind. Living with others isn't difficult for you, in fact it's essential. Since you are so adaptable you fit in easily to almost any environment, though you will always ultimately stamp your own character onto it. You love to be loved and offer a great deal in return, even if you are occasionally absent when people need you the most. In essence you are in love with life and so perhaps you should not be too surprised to discover that it is very fond of you too.

14

AQUARIUS ON THE CUSP

Astrological profiles are altered for those people born at either the beginning or the end of a zodiac sign, or, more properly, on the cusps of a sign. In the case of Aquarius this would be on the 21st of January and for two or three days after, and similarly at the end of the sign, probably from the 17th to the 19th of February.

The Capricorn Cusp – January 21st to 23rd

What really sets you apart is a genuinely practical streak that isn't always present in the sign of Aquarius when taken alone. You are likely to have all the joy of life and much of the devil-may-care attitude of your Sun sign, but at the same time you are capable of getting things done in a very positive way. This makes you likely to achieve a higher degree of material success and means that you ally managerial skills with the potential for rolling up your sleeves and taking part in the 'real work' yourself. Alongside this you are able to harness the naturally intuitive qualities of Aquarius in a very matter-of-fact way. Few people would have the ability to pull the wool over your eyes and you are rarely stuck for a solution, even to apparently difficult problems.

You express yourself less well than Aquarius taken alone, and you may have a sort of reserve that leads others to believe that your mind is full of still waters which run very deep. The air of mystery can actually be quite useful, because it masks an ability to react and move quickly when necessary, which is a great surprise to the people around you. However, there are two sides to every coin and if there is a slightly negative quality to this cuspid position it might lie in the fact that you are not quite the communicator that tends to be the case with Aquarius, and you could go through some fairly quiet and introspective phases that those around you would find somewhat difficult to understand. In a positive sense this offers a fairly wistful aspect to your nature that may, in romantic applications, appear very attractive. There is something deeply magnetic about your nature and it isn't quite possible for everyone to understand what makes you tick. Actually this is part of your appeal because there is nothing like curiosity on the part of others to enhance your profile.

Getting things done is what matters the most to you, harnessed to the ability to see the wider picture in life. It's true that not everyone understands your complex nature, but in friendship you are scarcely short of supportive types. Family members can be especially important to you and personal attachments are invariably made for life.

The Pisces Cusp – February 17th to 19th

It appears that you are more of a thinker than most and achieve depths of contemplation that would be totally alien to some signs of the zodiac. Much of your life is given over to the service you show for humanity as a whole but you don't sink into the depths of despair in the way that some Piscean individuals are inclined to do. You are immensely likeable and rarely stuck for a good idea. You know how to enjoy yourself, even if this quality is usually tied to the support and assistance that you constantly give to those around you.

Many of you will already have chosen a profession that somehow fulfils your need to be of service, and it isn't unusual for Pisces-cusp Aquarians to alter their path in life totally if it isn't fulfilling this most basic requirement. When necessary, you can turn your hand to almost anything, generally giving yourself totally to the task in hand, sometimes to the exclusion of everything else. People with this combination often have two very different sorts of career, sometimes managing to do both at the same time. Confidence in practical matters isn't usually lacking, even if you sometimes think that your thought processes are a little bit muddled.

In love you are ardent and more sincere than Aquarius sometimes seems to be. There can be a tinge of jealousy at work now and again in deep relationships, but you are less likely than Pisces to let this show. You tend to be very protective of the people who are most important in your life and these are probably fewer in number than often seems to be the case for Aquarius. Your love of humanity and the needs it has of you are of supreme importance and you barely let a day pass without offering some sort of assistance. For this reason, and many others, you are a much loved individual and show your most caring face to the world for the majority of your life. Material success can be hard to come by at first, but it isn't really an aspect of life that worries you too much in any case. It is far more important for you to be content with your lot and, if you are happy, it seems that more or less everything else tends to follow.

AQUARIUS AND ITS ASCENDANTS

The nature of every individual on the planet is composed of the rich variety of zodiac signs and planetary positions that were present at the time of their birth. Your Sun sign, which in your case is Aquarius, is one of the many factors when it comes to assessing the unique person you are. Probably the most important consideration, other than your Sun sign, is to establish the zodiac sign that was rising over the eastern horizon at the time that you were born. This is your Ascending or Rising sign. Most popular astrology fails to take account of the Ascendant, and yet its importance remains with you from the very moment of your birth, through every day of your life. The Ascendant is evident in the way you approach the world, and so, when meeting a person for the first time, it is this astrological influence that you are most likely to notice first. Our Ascending sign essentially represents what we appear to be, while the Sun sign is what we feel inside ourselves.

The Ascendant also has the potential for modifying our overall nature. For example, if you were born at a time of day when Aquarius was passing over the eastern horizon (this would be around the time of dawn) then you would be classed as a double Aquarian. As such, you would typify this zodiac sign, both internally and in your dealings with others. However, if your Ascendant sign turned out to be a Fire sign, such as Aries, there would be a profound alteration of nature, away from the expected qualities of Aquarius.

One of the reasons why popular astrology often ignores the Ascendant is that it has always been rather difficult to establish. We have found a way to make this possible by devising an easy-to-use table, which you will find on page 157 of this book. Using this, you can establish your Ascendant sign at a glance. You will need to know your rough time of birth, then it is simply a case of following the instructions.

For those readers who have no idea of their time of birth it might be worth allowing a good friend, or perhaps your partner, to read through the section that follows this introduction. Someone who deals with you on a regular basis may easily discover your Ascending sign, even though you could have some difficulty establishing it for yourself. A good understanding of this component of your nature is essential if you want to be aware of that 'other person' who is responsible for the way you make contact with the world at large. Your Sun sign, Ascendant sign, and the other pointers in this book will, together, allow you a far better understanding of what makes you tick as an individual. Peeling back the different layers of your astrological make-up can be an enlightening experience, and the Ascendant may represent one of the most important layers of all.

Aquarius with Aquarius Ascendant

You are totally unique and quite original, so much so that very few people could claim to understand what makes you tick. Routines get on your nerves and you need to be out there doing something most of the time. Getting where you want to go in life isn't too difficult, except that when you arrive, your destination might not look half so interesting as it did before. You are well liked and should have many friends. This is not to say that your pals have much in common with each other, because you choose from a wide cross-section of people. Although folks see you as being very reasonable in the main, you are capable of being quite cranky on occasions. Your intuition is extremely strong and is far less likely to let you down than would be the case with some individuals.

Travel is very important to you and you will probably live for some time in a different part of your own country, or even in another part of the world. At work you are more than capable, but do need something to do that you find personally stimulating, because you are not very good at constant routine. You can be relied upon to use your originality and find solutions that are instinctive and brilliant. Most people are very fond of you.

Aquarius with Pisces Ascendant

Here we find the originality of Aquarius balanced by the very sensitive qualities of Pisces, and it makes for a very interesting combination. When it comes to understanding other people you are second to none, but it's certain that you are more instinctive than either Pisces or Aquarius when taken alone. You are better at routines than Aquarius, but also relish a challenge more than the typical Piscean would. Active and enterprising, you tend to know what you want from life, but consideration of others, and the world at large, will always be part of the scenario. People with this combination often work on behalf of humanity and are to be found in social work, the medical profession and religious institutions. As far as beliefs are concerned you don't conform to established patterns, and yet may get closer to the truth of the Creator than many deep theological thinkers have ever been able to do. Acting on impulse as much as you do means that not everyone understands the way your mind works, but your popularity will invariably see you through.

Passionate and deeply sensitive, you are able to negotiate the twists and turns of a romantic life that is hardly likely to be run-of-the-mill. In the end, however, you should be able to discover a very deep personal and spiritual happiness.

Aquarius with Aries Ascendant

If ever anyone could be accused of setting off immediately, but slowly, it has to be you. These are very contradictory signs and the differences will express themselves in a variety of ways. One thing is certain, you have tremendous tenacity and will see a job through patiently from beginning to end, without tiring on the way and ensuring that every detail is taken care of properly. This combination often brings good health and a great capacity for continuity, particularly in terms of the length of life. You are certainly not as argumentative as the typical Aries, but you do know how to get your own way, which is just as well because you are usually thinking on behalf of everyone else and not just on your own account.

At home you can relax, which is a blessing for Aries, though in fact you seldom choose to do so because you always have some project or other on the go. You probably enjoy knocking down and rebuilding walls, though this is a practical tendency and not responsive to relationships, in which you are ardent and sincere. Impetuosity is as close to your heart as is the case for any type of subject, though you certainly have the ability to appear patient and steady. But it's just a front, isn't it?

Aquarius with Taurus Ascendant

There is nothing that you fail to think about deeply and with great intensity. You are wise, honest and very scientific in your approach to life. Routines are necessary in life but you have most of them sorted out well in advance and so always have time to look at the next interesting fact. If you don't spend all your time watching documentaries on the television set, you make a good friend and love to socialise. Most of the great discoveries of the world were probably made by people with this sort of astrological combination, though your nature is rather 'odd' on occasions and so can be rather difficult for others to understand.

You may be most surprised when others tell you that you are eccentric, but you don't really mind too much because for half of the time you are not inhabiting the same world as the rest of us. Because you can be delightfully dotty you are probably much loved and cherished by your friends, of which there are likely to be many. Family members probably adore you too, and you can be guaranteed to entertain anyone with whom you come into contact. The only fly in the ointment is that you sometimes lose track of reality, whatever that might be, and fly high in your own atmosphere of rarefied possibilities.

Aquarius with Gemini Ascendant

If you were around in the 1960s there is every chance that you were the first to go around with flowers in your hair. You are unconventional, original, quirky and entertaining. Few people would fail to notice your presence and you take life as it comes, even though on most occasions you are firmly in the driving seat. It all probability you care very much about the planet on which you live and the people with whom you share it. Not everyone understands you, but that does not really matter, for you have more than enough communication skills to put your message across intact. You should avoid wearing yourself out by worrying about things that you cannot control, and you definitely gain from taking time out to meditate. However, whether or not you allow yourself that luxury remains to be seen.

If you are not the most communicative form of Gemini subject then you must come a close second. Despite this fact much of what you have to say makes real sense and you revel in the company of interesting, intelligent and stimulating people, whose opinions on a host of matters will add to your own considerations. You are a true original in every sense of the word and the mere fact of your presence in the world is bound to add to the enjoyment of life experienced by the many people with whom you make contact.

Aquarius with Cancer Ascendant

The truly original spark, for which the sign of Aquarius is famed, can only enhance the caring qualities of Cancer, and is also inclined to bring the Crab out of its shell to a much greater extent than would be the case with certain other zodiac combinations. Aquarius is a party animal and never arrives without something interesting to say, which is doubly the case when the reservoir of emotion and consideration that is Cancer is feeding the tap. Your nature can be rather confusing for even you to deal with, but you are inspirational, bright, charming and definitely fun to be around.

The Cancer element in your nature means that you care about your home and the people to whom you are related. You are also a good and loyal friend, who would keep attachments for much longer than could be expected for Aquarius alone. You love to travel and can be expected to make many journeys to far-off places during your life. Some attention will have to be paid to your health, because you are capable of burning up masses of nervous energy, often without getting the periods of rest and contemplation that are essential to the deeper qualities of the sign of Cancer. Nevertheless you have determination, resilience and a refreshing attitude that lifts the spirits of the people in your vicinity.

Aquarius with Leo Ascendant

All associations with Aquarius bring originality, and you are no exception. You aspire to do your best most of the time but manage to achieve your objectives in an infinitely amusing and entertaining way. Not that you set out to do so, because if you are an actor on the stage of life, it seems as though you are a natural one. There is nothing remotely pretentious about your breezy personality or your ability to occupy the centre of any stage. This analogy is quite appropriate because you probably like the theatre. Being in any situation when reality is suspended for a while suits you down to the ground, and in any case you may regularly ask yourself if you even recognise what reality is. Always asking questions, both of yourself and the world at large, you soldier on relentlessly, though not to the exclusion of having a good time on the way.

Keeping to tried and tested paths is not your way. You are a natural trailblazer who is full of good ideas and who has the energy to put them into practice. You care deeply for the people who play an important part in your life but are wise enough to allow them the space they need to develop their own personalities along the way. Most people like you, many love you, and one or two think that you really are the best thing since sliced bread.

Aquarius with Virgo Ascendant

How could anyone make the convention unconventional? Well, if anyone can manage, you can. There are great contradictions here, because on the one hand you always want to do the expected thing, but the Aquarian quality within your nature loves to surprise everyone on the way. If you don't always know what you are thinking or doing, it's a pretty safe bet that others won't either, so it's important on occasions really to stop and think. However this is not a pressing concern, because you tend to live a fairly happy life and muddle through no matter what. Other people tend to take to you well and it is likely that you will have many friends. You tend to be bright and cheerful and can approach even difficult tasks with the certainty that you have the skills necessary to see them through to their conclusion. Give and take are important factors in the life of any individual and particularly so in your case. Because you can stretch yourself in order to understand what makes other people think and act in the way that they do, you have the reputation of being a good friend and a reliable colleague.

In love you can be somewhat more fickle than the typical Virgoan, and yet you are always interesting to live with. Where you are, things happen, and you mix a sparkling wit with deep insights.

Aquarius with Libra Ascendant

Stand by for a truly interesting and very inspiring combination here, but one that is sometimes rather difficult to fathom, even for the sort of people who believe themselves to be very perceptive. The reason for this could be that any situation has to be essentially fixed and constant in order to get a handle on it, and this is certainly not the case for the Aquarian–Libran type. The fact is that both these signs are Air signs, and to a certain extent as unpredictable as the wind itself.

To most people you seem to be original, frank, free and very outspoken. Not everything you do makes sense to others and if you were alive during the hippy era, it is likely that you went around with flowers in your hair, for you are a free-thinking idealist at heart. With age you mature somewhat, but never too much, because you will always see the strange, the comical and the original in life. This is what keeps you young and is one of the factors that makes you so very attractive to members of the opposite sex. Many people will want to 'adopt' you and you are at your very best when in company. Much of your effort is expounded on others and yet, unless you discipline yourself a good deal, personal relationships of the romantic sort can bring certain difficulties. Careful planning is necessary.

Aquarius with Scorpio Ascendant

Here we have a combination that shows much promise and a flexibility that allows many changes in direction, allied to a power to succeed, sometimes very much against all the odds. Aquarius lightens the load of the Scorpio mind, turning the depths into potential, and intuitive foresight into a means for getting on in life. There are depths here, because even airy Aquarius isn't so easy to understand, and it is therefore a fact that some people with this combination will always be something of a mystery. However, even this fact can be turned to your advantage because it means that people will always be looking at you. Confidence is so often the key to success in life and the Scorpio–Aquarius mix offers this, or at least appears to do so. Even when this is not entirely the case, the fact that everyone around you believes it to be true is often enough.

You are usually good to know, and show a keen intellect and a deep intelligence, aided by a fascination for life that knows no bounds. When at your best you are giving, understanding, balanced and active. On those occasions when things are not going well for you, beware of a stubborn streak and the need to be sensational. Keep it light and happy and you won't go far wrong. Most of you are very, very much loved.

Aquarius with Sagittarius Ascendant

There is an original streak to your nature which is very attractive to the people with whom you share your life. Always different, ever on the go and anxious to try out the next experiment in life, you are interested in almost everything, and yet deeply attached to almost nothing. Everyone you know thinks that you are a little 'odd', but you probably don't mind them believing this because you know it to be true. In fact it is possible that you positively relish your eccentricity, which sets you apart from the common herd and means that you are always going to be noticed.

Although it may seem strange with this combination of Air and Fire, you can be distinctly cool on occasions, have a deep and abiding love of your own company now and again and won't be easily understood. Love comes fairly easily to you but there are times when you are accused of being self-possessed, self-indulgent and not willing enough to fall in line with the wishes of those around you. Despite this you walk on and on down your own path. At heart you are an extrovert and you love to party, often late into the night. Luxury appeals to you, though it tends to be of the transient sort. Travel could easily play a major and a very important part in your life.

Aquarius with Capricorn Ascendant

Here the determination of Capricorn is assisted by a slightly more adaptable quality and an off-beat personality that tends to keep everyone else guessing. You don't care to be quite so predictable as the archetypal Capricorn would be, and there is a more idealistic quality here, or at least one that shows more. A greater number of friends than Capricorn usually keeps is likely, though less than the true Aquarian would gather. Few people doubt your sincerity, though by no means all of them understand what makes you tick. Unfortunately you are not in a position to help them out, because you are not too sure yourself. All the same, you muddle through and can be very capable when the mood takes you.

Being a natural traveller, you love to see new places and would be quite fascinated by cultures that are very different to your own. People with this combination are inclined to spend some time living abroad and may even settle there. You look out for the underdog and will always have time for a good cause, no matter what it takes to help. In romantic terms you are a reliable partner, though with a slightly wayward edge which, if anything, tends to make you even more attractive. Listen to your intuition, which is well honed and rarely lets you down. Generally speaking you are very popular.

THE MOON AND THE PART IT PLAYS IN YOUR LIFE

In astrology the Moon is probably the single most important heavenly body after the Sun. Its unique position, as partner to the Earth on its journey around the solar system, means that the Moon appears to pass through the signs of the zodiac extremely quickly. The zodiac position of the Moon at the time of your birth plays a great part in personal character and is especially significant in the build-up of your emotional nature.

Your Own Moon Sign

Discovering the position of the Moon at the time of your birth has always been notoriously difficult because tracking the complex zodiac positions of the Moon is not easy. This process has been reduced to three simple stages with our Lunar Tables. A breakdown of the Moon's zodiac positions can be found from page 35 onwards, so that once you know what your Moon Sign is, you can see what part this plays in the overall build-up of your personal character.

If you follow the instructions on the next page you will soon be able to work out exactly what zodiac sign the Moon occupied on the day that you were born and you can then go on to compare the reading for this position with those of your Sun sign and your Ascendant. It is partly the comparison between these three important positions that goes towards making you the unique individual you are.

31

HOW TO DISCOVER YOUR MOON SIGN

This is a three-stage process. You may need a pen and a piece of paper but if you follow the instructions below the process should only take a minute or so.

STAGE 1 First of all you need to know the Moon Age at the time of your birth. If you look at Moon Table 1, on page 33, you will find all the years between 1917 and 2015 down the left side. Find the year of your birth and then trace across to the right to the month of your birth. Where the two intersect you will find a number. This is the date of the New Moon in the month that you were born. You now need to count forward the number of days between the New Moon and your own birthday. For example, if the New Moon in the month of your birth was shown as being the 6th and you were born on the 20th, your Moon Age Day would be 14. If the New Moon in the month of your birth came after your birthday, you need to count forward from the New Moon in the previous month, which, if you were born in January, means you must look at December in the previous year. You cannot count from December in the year of your birth, as that month is *after* your birth. Whatever the result, jot this number down so that you do not forget it.

STAGE 2 Take a look at Moon Table 2 on page 34. Down the left hand column look for the date of your birth. Now trace across to the month of your birth. Where the two meet you will find a letter. Copy this letter down alongside your Moon Age Day.

STAGE 3 Moon Table 3 on page 34 will supply you with the zodiac sign the Moon occupied on the day of your birth. Look for your Moon Age Day down the left hand column and then for the letter you found in Stage 2. Where the two converge you will find a zodiac sign and this is the sign occupied by the Moon on the day that you were born.

Your Zodiac Moon Sign Explained

You will find a profile of all zodiac Moon Signs on pages 35 to 38, showing in yet another way how astrology helps to make you into the individual that you are. In each daily entry of the Astral Diary you can find the zodiac position of the Moon for every day of the year. This also allows you to discover your lunar birthdays. Since the Moon passes through all the signs of the zodiac in about a month, you can expect something like twelve lunar birthdays each year. At these times you are likely to be emotionally steady and able to make the sort of decisions that have real, lasting value.

MOON TABLE 1

YEAR	DEC	JAN	FEB	YEAR	DEC	JAN	FEB	YEAR	DEC	JAN	FEB
1917	13	24	22	1950	9	18	16	1983	4	14	13
1918	2	12	11	1951	28	7	6	1984	22	3	1
1919	21	1/31	–	1952	17	26	25	1985	12	21	19
1920	10	20	19	1953	6	15	14	1986	1/30	10	9
1921	29	9	8	1954	25	5	3	1987	20	29	28
1922	18	27	26	1955	14	24	22	1988	9	19	17
1923	8	17	15	1956	2	13	11	1989	28	7	6
1924	26	6	5	1957	21	1/30	–	1990	17	26	25
1925	15	24	23	1958	10	19	18	1991	6	15	14
1926	5	14	12	1959	29	9	7	1992	24	4	3
1927	24	3	2	1960	18	27	26	1993	14	23	22
1928	12	21	19	1961	7	16	15	1994	2	11	10
1929	1/30	11	9	1962	26	6	5	1995	22	1/30	–
1930	19	29	28	1963	15	25	23	1996	10	20	18
1931	9	18	17	1964	4	14	13	1997	28	9	7
1932	27	7	6	1965	22	3	1	1998	18	27	26
1933	17	25	24	1966	12	21	19	1999	7	17	16
1934	6	15	14	1967	1/30	10	9	2000	26	6	4
1935	25	5	3	1968	20	29	28	2001	15	25	23
1936	13	24	22	1969	9	19	17	2002	4	13	12
1937	2	12	11	1970	28	7	6	2003	23	3	1
1938	21	1/31	–	1971	17	26	25	2004	11	21	20
1939	10	20	19	1972	6	15	14	2005	30	10	9
1940	28	9	8	1973	25	5	4	2006	20	29	28
1941	18	27	26	1974	14	24	22	2007	9	18	16
1942	8	16	15	1975	3	12	11	2008	27	8	6
1943	27	6	4	1976	21	1/31	29	2009	16	26	25
1944	15	25	24	1977	10	19	18	2010	6	15	14
1945	4	14	12	1978	29	9	7	2011	25	4	3
1946	23	3	2	1979	18	27	26	2012	12	23	22
1947	12	21	19	1980	7	16	15	2013	2	12	10
1948	1/30	11	9	1981	26	6	4	2014	2	1/31	–
1949	19	29	27	1982	15	25	23	2015	20	19	20

22

TABLE 2   MOON TABLE 3

DAY	JAN	FEB	M/D	A	B	C	D	E	F	G
1	A	D	0	CP	AQ	AQ	AQ	PI	PI	PI
2	A	D	1	AQ	AQ	AQ	PI	PI	PI	AR
3	A	D	2	AQ	AQ	PI	PI	PI	AR	AR
4	A	D	3	AQ	PI	PI	PI	AR	AR	AR
5	A	D	4	PI	PI	AR	AR	AR	AR	TA
6	A	D	5	PI	AR	AR	AR	TA	TA	TA
7	A	D	6	AR	AR	AR	TA	TA	TA	GE
8	A	D	7	AR	AR	TA	TA	TA	GE	GE
9	A	D	8	AR	TA	TA	TA	GE	GE	GE
10	A	E	9	TA	TA	GE	GE	GE	CA	CA
11	B	E	10	TA	GE	GE	GE	CA	CA	CA
12	B	E	11	GE	GE	GE	CA	CA	CA	LE
13	B	E	12	GE	GE	CA	CA	CA	LE	LE
14	B	E	13	GE	CA	CA	LE	LE	LE	LE
15	B	E	14	CA	CA	LE	LE	LE	VI	VI
16	B	E	15	CA	LE	LE	LE	VI	VI	VI
17	B	E	16	LE	LE	LE	VI	VI	VI	LI
18	B	E	17	LE	LE	VI	VI	VI	LI	LI
19	B	E	18	LE	VI	VI	VI	LI	LI	LI
20	B	F	19	VI	VI	VI	LI	LI	LI	SC
21	C	F	20	VI	LI	LI	LI	SC	SC	SC
22	C	F	21	LI	LI	LI	SC	SC	SC	SA
23	C	F	22	LI	LI	SC	SC	SC	SA	SA
24	C	F	23	LI	SC	SC	SC	SA	SA	SA
25	C	F	24	SC	SC	SC	SA	SA	SA	CP
26	C	F	25	SC	SA	SA	SA	CP	CP	CP
27	C	F	26	SA	SA	SA	CP	CP	CP	AQ
28	C	F	27	SA	SA	CP	CP	AQ	AQ	AQ
29	C	F	28	SA	CP	CP	AQ	AQ	AQ	AQ
30	C	–	29	CP	CP	CP	AQ	AQ	AQ	PI
31	D	–								

AR = Aries, TA = Taurus, GE = Gemini, CA = Cancer, LE = Leo, VI = Virgo,
LI = Libra, SC = Scorpio, SA – Sagittarius, CP = Capricorn, AQ = Aquarius, PI = Pisces

MOON SIGNS

Moon in Aries

You have a strong imagination, courage, determination and a desire to do things in your own way and forge your own path through life.

Originality is a key attribute; you are seldom stuck for ideas although your mind is changeable and you could take the time to focus on individual tasks. Often quick-tempered, you take orders from few people and live life at a fast pace. Avoid health problems by taking regular time out for rest and relaxation.

Emotionally, it is important that you talk to those you are closest to and work out your true feelings. Once you discover that people are there to help, there is less necessity for you to do everything yourself.

Moon in Taurus

The Moon in Taurus gives you a courteous and friendly manner, which means you are likely to have many friends.

The good things in life mean a lot to you, as Taurus is an Earth sign that delights in experiences which please the senses. Hence you are probably a lover of good food and drink, which may in turn mean you need to keep an eye on the bathroom scales, especially as looking good is also important to you.

Emotionally you are fairly stable and you stick by your own standards. Taureans do not respond well to change. Intuition also plays an important part in your life.

Moon in Gemini

You have a warm-hearted character, sympathetic and eager to help others. At times reserved, you can also be articulate and chatty: this is part of the paradox of Gemini, which always brings duplicity to the nature. You are interested in current affairs, have a good intellect, and are good company and likely to have many friends. Most of your friends have a high opinion of you and would be ready to defend you should the need arise. However, this is usually unnecessary, as you are quite capable of defending yourself in any verbal confrontation.

Travel is important to your inquisitive mind and you find intellectual stimulus in mixing with people from different cultures. You also gain much from reading, writing and the arts but you do need plenty of rest and relaxation in order to avoid fatigue.

Moon in Cancer

The Moon in Cancer at the time of birth is a fortunate position as Cancer is the Moon's natural home. This means that the qualities of compassion and understanding given by the Moon are especially enhanced in your nature, and you are friendly and sociable and cope well with emotional pressures. You cherish home and family life, and happily do the domestic tasks. Your surroundings are important to you and you hate squalor and filth. You are likely to have a love of music and poetry.

Your basic character, although at times changeable like the Moon itself, depends on symmetry. You aim to make your surroundings comfortable and harmonious, for yourself and those close to you.

Moon in Leo

The best qualities of the Moon and Leo come together to make you warm-hearted, fair, ambitious and self-confident. With good organisational abilities, you invariably rise to a position of responsibility in your chosen career. This is fortunate as you don't enjoy being an 'also-ran' and would rather be an important part of a small organisation than a menial in a large one.

You should be lucky in love, and happy, provided you put in the effort to make a comfortable home for yourself and those close to you. It is likely that you will have a love of pleasure, sport, music and literature. Life brings you many rewards, most of them as a direct result of your own efforts, although you may be luckier than average and ready to make the best of any situation.

Moon in Virgo

You are endowed with good mental abilities and a keen receptive memory, but you are never ostentatious or pretentious. Naturally quite reserved, you still have many friends, especially of the opposite sex. Marital relationships must be discussed carefully and worked at so that they remain harmonious, as personal attachments can be a problem if you do not give them your full attention.

Talented and persevering, you possess artistic qualities and are a good homemaker. Earning your honours through genuine merit, you work long and hard towards your objectives but show little pride in your achievements. Many short journeys will be undertaken in your life.

Moon in Libra

With the Moon in Libra you are naturally popular and make friends easily. People like you, probably more than you realise, you bring fun to a party and are a natural diplomat. For all its good points, Libra is not the most stable of astrological signs and, as a result, your emotions can be a little unstable too. Therefore, although the Moon in Libra is said to be good for love and marriage, your Sun sign and Rising sign will have an important effect on your emotional and loving qualities.

You must remember to relate to others in your decision-making. Co-operation is crucial because Libra represents the 'balance' of life that can only be achieved through harmonious relationships. Conformity is not easy for you because Libra, an Air sign, likes its independence.

Moon in Scorpio

Some people might call you pushy. In fact, all you really want to do is to live life to the full and protect yourself and your family from the pressures of life. Take care to avoid giving the impression of being sarcastic or impulsive and use your energies wisely and constructively.

You have great courage and you invariably achieve your goals by force of personality and sheer effort. You are fond of mystery and are good at predicting the outcome of situations and events. Travel experiences can be beneficial to you.

You may experience problems if you do not take time to examine your motives in a relationship, and also if you allow jealousy, always a feature of Scorpio, to cloud your judgement.

Moon in Sagittarius

The Moon in Sagittarius helps to make you a generous individual with humanitarian qualities and a kind heart. Restlessness may be intrinsic as your mind is seldom still. Perhaps because of this, you have a need for change that could lead you to several major moves during your adult life. You are not afraid to stand your ground when you know your judgement is right, you speak directly and have good intuition.

At work you are quick, efficient and versatile and so you make an ideal employee. You need work to be intellectually demanding and do not enjoy tedious routines.

In relationships, you anger quickly if faced with stupidity or deception, though you are just as quick to forgive and forget. Emotionally, there are times when your heart rules your head.

37

Moon in Capricorn

The Moon in Capricorn makes you popular and likely to come into the public eye in some way. The watery Moon is not entirely comfortable in the Earth sign of Capricorn and this may lead to some difficulties in the early years of life. An initial lack of creative ability and indecision must be overcome before the true qualities of patience and perseverance inherent in Capricorn can show through.

You have good administrative ability and are a capable worker, and if you are careful you can accumulate wealth. But you must be cautious and take professional advice in partnerships, as you are open to deception. You may be interested in social or welfare work, which suit your organisational skills and sympathy for others.

Moon in Aquarius

The Moon in Aquarius makes you an active and agreeable person with a friendly, easy-going nature. Sympathetic to the needs of others, you flourish in a laid-back atmosphere. You are broad-minded, fair and open to suggestion, although sometimes you have an unconventional quality which others can find hard to understand.

You are interested in the strange and curious, and in old articles and places. You enjoy trips to these places and gain much from them. Political, scientific and educational work interests you and you might choose a career in science or technology.

Money-wise, you make gains through innovation and concentration and Lunar Aquarians often tackle more than one job at a time. In love you are kind and honest.

Moon in Pisces

You have a kind, sympathetic nature, somewhat retiring at times, but you always take account of others' feelings and help when you can.

Personal relationships may be problematic, but as life goes on you can learn from your experiences and develop a better understanding of yourself and the world around you.

You have a fondness for travel, appreciate beauty and harmony and hate disorder and strife. You may be fond of literature and would make a good writer or speaker yourself. You have a creative imagination and may come across as an incurable romantic. You have strong intuition, maybe bordering on a mediumistic quality, which sets you apart from the mass. You may not be rich in cash terms, but your personal gifts are worth more than gold.

AQUARIUS IN LOVE

Discover how compatible in love you are with people from the same and other signs of the zodiac. Five stars equals a match made in heaven!

Aquarius meets Aquarius

This is a good match for several reasons. Most importantly, although it sounds arrogant, Aquarians like themselves. At its best, Aquarius is one of the fairest, most caring and genuinely pleasant zodiac signs and so it is only when faced by the difficulties created by others that it shows a less favourable side. Put two Aquarians together and voilà – instant success! Personal and family life should bring more joy. On the whole, a platform for adventure based on solid foundations. Star rating: *****

Aquarius meets Pisces

Zodiac signs that follow each other often have something in common, but this is not the case with Aquarius and Pisces. Both signs are deeply caring, but in different ways. Pisces is one of the deepest zodiac signs, and Aquarius simply isn't prepared to embark on the journey. Pisceans, meanwhile, would probably find Aquarians superficial and even flippant. On the positive side there is potential for a well-balanced relationship, but unless one party is untypical of their zodiac sign, it often doesn't get started. Star rating: **

Aquarius meets Aries

Aquarius is an Air sign, and Air and Fire often work well together, but not in the case of Aries and Aquarius. The average Aquarian lives in what the Ram sees as a fantasy world, so a meeting of minds is unlikely. Of course, the dominant side of Aries could be trained by the devil-may-care attitude of Aquarius. There are meeting points but they are difficult to establish. However, given sufficient time and an open mind on both sides, a degree of happiness is possible. Star rating: **

Aquarius meets Taurus

In any relationship of which Aquarius is a part, surprises abound. It is difficult for Taurus to understand the soul-searching, adventurous, changeable Aquarian, but on the positive side, the Bull is adaptable and can respond well to a dose of excitement. Aquarians are kind and react well to the same quality coming back at them. Both are friendly, capable of deep affection and basically creative. Unfortunately, Taurus simply doesn't know what makes Aquarius tick, which could lead to feelings of isolation, even if these don't always show on the surface. Star rating: **

Aquarius meets Gemini

Aquarius is commonly mistaken for a Water sign, but in fact it's ruled by the Air element, and this is the key to its compatibility with Gemini. Both signs mix freely socially, and each has an insatiable curiosity. There is plenty of action, lots of love, but very little rest, and so great potential for success if they don't wear each other out! Aquarius revels in its own eccentricity, and encourages Gemini to emulate this. Theirs will be an unconventional household, but almost everyone warms to this crazy and unpredictable couple. Star rating: *****

Aquarius meets Cancer

Cancer is often attracted to Aquarius and, as Aquarius is automatically on the side of anyone who fancies it, so there is the potential for something good here. Cancer loves Aquarius' devil-may-care approach to life, but also recognises and seeks to strengthen the basic lack of self-confidence that all Air signs try so hard to keep secret. Both signs are natural travellers and are quite adventurous. Their family life could be unusual, but friends would recognise a caring, sharing household with many different interests shared by people genuinely in love. Star rating: ***

Aquarius meets Leo

The problem here is that Aquarius doesn't think in the general sense of the word, it knows. Leo, on the other hand, is more practical and relies more on logical reasoning, and consequently it doesn't understand Aquarius very well. Aquarians can also appear slightly frosty in their appreciation of others and this, too, will annoy Leo. This is a good match for a business partnership because Aquarius is astute, while Leo is brave, but personally the prognosis is less promising. Tolerance, understanding and forbearance are all needed to make this work. Star rating: **

Aquarius meets Virgo

Aquarius is a strange sign because no matter how well one knows it, it always manages to surprise. For this reason, against the odds, it's quite likely that Aquarius will form a sucessful relationship with Virgo. Aquarius is changeable, unpredictable and often quite odd, while Virgo is steady, a fuss-pot and very practical. Herein lies the key. What one sign needs, the other provides and that may be the surest recipe for success imaginable. On-lookers may not know why the couple are happy, but they will recognise that this is the case. Star rating: ****

Aquarius meets Libra

One of the best combinations imaginable, partly because both are Air signs and so share a common meeting point. But perhaps the more crucial factor is that both signs respect each other. Aquarius loves life and originality, and is quite intellectual. Libra is similar, but more balanced and rather less eccentric. A visit to this couple's house would be entertaining and full of zany wit, activity and excitement. Both are keen to travel and may prefer to 'find themselves' before taking on too many domestic responsibilities. Star rating: *****

Aquarius meets Scorpio

This is a promising and practical combination. Scorpio responds well to Aquarius' persistent exploration of its deep nature and so this generally shy sign becomes lighter, brighter and more inspirational. Meanwhile, Aquarians are rarely as sure of themselves as they like to appear and are reassured by Scorpio's constant, steady and determined support. Both signs want to be kind to each other, which is a good starting point to a relationship that should be warm most of the time and extremely hot occasionally. Star rating: ****

Aquarius meets Sagittarius

Both Sagittarius and Aquarius are into mind games, which may lead to something of an intellectual competition. If one side is happy to be 'bamboozled' it won't be a problem, but it is more likely that the relationship will turn into a competition, which won't auger well for its long-term future. However, on the plus side, both signs are adventurous and sociable, so as long as there is always something new and interesting to do, the match could turn out very well. Star rating: **

Aquarius meets Capricorn

Probably one of the least likely combinations, as Capricorn and Aquarius are unlikely to choose each other in the first place, unless one side is quite untypical of their sign. Capricorn approaches things in a practical way and likes to get things done, while Aquarius works almost exclusively for the moment and relies heavily on intuition. Their attitudes to romance are also diametrically opposed: Aquarius' moods tend to swing from red hot to ice cold in a minute, which is alien to steady Capricorn. Star rating: **

VENUS:
THE PLANET OF LOVE

If you look up at the sky around sunset or sunrise you will often see Venus in close attendance to the Sun. It is arguably one of the most beautiful sights of all and there is little wonder that historically it became associated with the goddess of love. But although Venus does play an important part in the way you view love and in the way others see you romantically, this is only one of the spheres of influence that it enjoys in your overall character.

Venus has a part to play in the more cultured side of your life and has much to do with your appreciation of art, literature, music and general creativity. Even the way you look is responsive to the part of the zodiac that Venus occupied at the start of your life, though this fact is also down to your Sun sign and Ascending sign. If, at the time you were born, Venus occupied one of the more gregarious zodiac signs, you will be more likely to wear your heart on your sleeve, as well as to be more attracted to entertainment, social gatherings and good company. If on the other hand Venus occupied a quiet zodiac sign at the time of your birth, you would tend to be more retiring and less willing to shine in public situations.

It's good to know what part the planet Venus plays in your life for it can have a great bearing on the way you appear to the rest of the world and since we all have to mix with others, you can learn to make the very best of what Venus has to offer you.

One of the great complications in the past has always been trying to establish exactly what zodiac position Venus enjoyed when you were born because the planet is notoriously difficult to track. However, we have solved that problem by creating a table that is exclusive to your Sun sign, which you will find on the following page.

Establishing your Venus sign could not be easier. Just look up the year of your birth on the following page and you will see a sign of the zodiac. This was the sign that Venus occupied in the period covered by your sign in that year. If Venus occupied more than one sign during the period, this is indicated by the date on which the sign changed, and the name of the new sign. For instance, if you were born in 1945, Venus was in Pisces until the 12th February, after which time it was in Aries. If you were born before 12th February your Venus sign is Pisces, if you were born on or after 12th February, your Venus sign is Aries. Once you have established the position of Venus at the time of your birth, you can then look in the pages which follow to see how this has a bearing on your life as a whole.

43

1917 CAPRICORN / 9.2 AQUARIUS
1918 AQUARIUS
1919 AQUARIUS / 3.2 PISCES
1920 SAGITTARIUS / 30.1 CAPRICORN
1921 PISCES / 15.2 ARIES
1922 CAPRICORN / 25.1 AQUARIUS /
   18.2 PISCES
1923 SAGITTARIUS / 7.2 CAPRICORN
1924 PISCES / 13.2 ARIES
1925 CAPRICORN / 9.2 AQUARIUS
1926 AQUARIUS
1927 AQUARIUS / 2.2 PISCES
1928 SAGITTARIUS / 29.1 CAPRICORN
1929 PISCES / 14.2 ARIES
1930 CAPRICORN / 25.1 AQUARIUS /
   18.2 PISCES
1931 SAGITTARIUS / 6.2 CAPRICORN
1932 PISCES / 13.2 ARIES
1933 CAPRICORN / 8.2 AQUARIUS
1934 AQUARIUS
1935 AQUARIUS / 2.2 PISCES
1936 SAGITTARIUS / 29.1 CAPRICORN
1937 PISCES / 13.2 ARIES
1938 CAPRICORN / 24.1 AQUARIUS /
   17.2 PISCES
1939 SAGITTARIUS / 6.2 CAPRICORN
1940 PISCES / 12.2 ARIES
1941 CAPRICORN / 8.2 AQUARIUS
1942 AQUARIUS
1943 AQUARIUS / 1.2 PISCES
1944 SAGITTARIUS / 28.1 CAPRICORN
1945 PISCES / 12.2 ARIES
1946 CAPRICORN / 24.1 AQUARIUS /
   17.2 PISCES
1947 SAGITTARIUS / 6.2 CAPRICORN
1948 PISCES / 12.2 ARIES
1949 CAPRICORN / 7.2 AQUARIUS
1950 AQUARIUS
1951 AQUARIUS / 1.2 PISCES
1952 SAGITTARIUS / 27.1 CAPRICORN
1953 PISCES / 11.2 ARIES
1954 CAPRICORN / 23.1 AQUARIUS /
   16.2 PISCES
1955 SAGITTARIUS / 6.2 CAPRICORN
1956 PISCES / 11.2 ARIES
1957 CAPRICORN / 7.2 AQUARIUS
1958 AQUARIUS
1959 AQUARIUS / 31.1 PISCES
1960 SAGITTARIUS / 27.1 CAPRICORN
1961 PISCES / 9.2 ARIES
1962 CAPRICORN / 23.1 AQUARIUS /
   15.2 PISCES
1963 SAGITTARIUS / 6.2 CAPRICORN
1964 PISCES / 11.2 ARIES

1965 CAPRICORN / 6.2 AQUARIUS
1966 AQUARIUS
1967 AQUARIUS / 30.1 PISCES
1968 SAGITTARIUS / 26.1 CAPRICORN
1969 PISCES / 7.2 ARIES
1970 CAPRICORN / 22.1 AQUARIUS /
   15.2 PISCES
1971 SAGITTARIUS / 5.2 CAPRICORN
1972 PISCES / 10.2 ARIES
1973 CAPRICORN / 5.2 AQUARIUS
1974 AQUARIUS / 7.2 CAPRICORN
1975 AQUARIUS / 30.1 PISCES
1976 SAGITTARIUS / 26.1 CAPRICORN
1977 PISCES / 5.2 ARIES
1978 CAPRICORN / 22.1 AQUARIUS /
   14.2 PISCES
1979 SAGITTARIUS / 5.2 CAPRICORN
1980 PISCES / 10.2 ARIES
1981 CAPRICORN / 5.2 AQUARIUS
1982 AQUARIUS / 29.1 CAPRICORN
1983 AQUARIUS / 29.1 PISCES
1984 SAGITTARIUS / 25.1 CAPRICORN
1985 PISCES / 5.2 ARIES
1986 AQUARIUS / 14.2 PISCES
1987 SAGITTARIUS / 5.2 CAPRICORN
1988 PISCES / 9.2 ARIES
1989 CAPRICORN / 4.2 AQUARIUS
1990 AQUARIUS / 23.1 CAPRICORN
1991 AQUARIUS / 29.1 PISCES
1992 SAGITTARIUS / 25.1 CAPRICORN
1993 PISCES / 4.2 ARIES
1994 AQUARIUS / 13.2 PISCES
1995 SAGITTARIUS / 5.2 CAPRICORN
1996 PISCES / 9.2 ARIES
1997 CAPRICORN / 4.2 AQUARIUS
1998 AQUARIUS / 23.1 CAPRICORN
1999 AQUARIUS / 29.1 PISCES
2000 SAGITTARIUS / 25.1 CAPRICORN
2001 PISCES / 4.2 ARIES
2002 AQUARIUS / 13.2 PISCES
2003 SAGITTARIUS
2004 PISCES / 9.2 AQUARIUS
2005 CAPRICORN / 6.2 AQUARIUS
2006 AQUARIUS / 14.01 CAPRICORN
2007 AQUARIUS / 19.01 PISCES
2008 SAGITTARIUS / 25.1 CAPRICORN
2009 PISCES / 4.2 ARIES
2010 AQUARIUS / 12.2 PISCES
2011 SAGITTARIUS
2012 PISCES / 9.2 AQUARIUS
2013 CAPRICORN / 6.2 AQUARIUS
2014 CAPRICORN / 6.2 AQUARIUS
2015 AQUARIUS / 29.1 PISCES

44

VENUS THROUGH THE ZODIAC SIGNS

Venus in Aries

Amongst other things, the position of Venus in Aries indicates a fondness for travel, music and all creative pursuits. Your nature tends to be affectionate and you would try not to create confusion or difficulty for others if it could be avoided. Many people with this planetary position have a great love of the theatre, and mental stimulation is of the greatest importance. Early romantic attachments are common with Venus in Aries, so it is very important to establish a genuine sense of romantic continuity. Early marriage is not recommended, especially if it is based on sympathy. You may give your heart a little too readily on occasions.

Venus in Taurus

You are capable of very deep feelings and your emotions tend to last for a very long time. This makes you a trusting partner and lover, whose constancy is second to none. In life you are precise and careful and always try to do things the right way. Although this means an ordered life, which you are comfortable with, it can also lead you to be rather too fussy for your own good. Despite your pleasant nature, you are very fixed in your opinions and quite able to speak your mind. Others are attracted to you and historical astrologers always quoted this position of Venus as being very fortunate in terms of marriage. However, if you find yourself involved in a failed relationship, it could take you a long time to trust again.

Venus in Gemini

As with all associations related to Gemini, you tend to be quite versatile, anxious for change and intelligent in your dealings with the world at large. You may gain money from more than one source but you are equally good at spending it. There is an inference here that you are a good communicator, via either the written or the spoken word, and you love to be in the company of interesting people. Always on the look-out for culture, you may also be very fond of music, and love to indulge the curious and cultured side of your nature. In romance you tend to have more than one relationship and could find yourself associated with someone who has previously been a friend or even a distant relative.

Venus in Cancer

You often stay close to home because you are very fond of family and enjoy many of your most treasured moments when you are with those you love. Being naturally sympathetic, you will always do anything you can to support those around you, even people you hardly know at all. This charitable side of your nature is your most noticeable trait and is one of the reasons why others are naturally so fond of you. Being receptive and in some cases even psychic, you can see through to the soul of most of those with whom you come into contact. You may not commence too many romantic attachments but when you do give your heart, it tends to be unconditionally.

Venus in Leo

It must become quickly obvious to almost anyone you meet that you are kind, sympathetic and yet determined enough to stand up for anyone or anything that is truly important to you. Bright and sunny, you warm the world with your natural enthusiasm and would rarely do anything to hurt those around you, or at least not intentionally. In romance you are ardent and sincere, though some may find your style just a little overpowering. Gains come through your contacts with other people and this could be especially true with regard to romance, for love and money often come hand in hand for those who were born with Venus in Leo. People claim to understand you, though you are more complex than you seem.

Venus in Virgo

Your nature could well be fairly quiet no matter what your Sun sign might be, though this fact often manifests itself as an inner peace and would not prevent you from being basically sociable. Some delays and even the odd disappointment in love cannot be ruled out with this planetary position, though it's a fact that you will usually find the happiness you look for in the end. Catapulting yourself into romantic entanglements that you know to be rather ill-advised is not sensible, and it would be better to wait before you committed yourself exclusively to any one person. It is the essence of your nature to serve the world at large and through doing so it is possible that you will attract money at some stage in your life.

Venus in Libra

Venus is very comfortable in Libra and bestows upon those people who have this planetary position a particular sort of kindness that is easy to recognise. This is a very good position for all sorts of friendships and also for romantic attachments that usually bring much joy into your life. Few individuals with Venus in Libra would avoid marriage and since you are capable of great depths of love, it is likely that you will find a contented personal life. You like to mix with people of integrity and intelligence but don't take kindly to scruffy surroundings or work that means getting your hands too dirty. Careful speculation, good business dealings and money through marriage all seem fairly likely.

Venus in Scorpio

You are quite open and tend to spend money quite freely, even on those occasions when you don't have very much. Although your intentions are always good, there are times when you get yourself in to the odd scrape and this can be particularly true when it comes to romance, which you may come to late or from a rather unexpected direction. Certainly you have the power to be happy and to make others contented on the way, but you find the odd stumbling block on your journey through life and it could seem that you have to work harder than those around you. As a result of this, you gain a much deeper understanding of the true value of personal happiness than many people ever do, and are likely to achieve true contentment in the end.

Venus in Sagittarius

You are lighthearted, cheerful and always able to see the funny side of any situation. These facts enhance your popularity, which is especially high with members of the opposite sex. You should never have to look too far to find romantic interest in your life, though it is just possible that you might be too willing to commit yourself before you are certain that the person in question is right for you. Part of the problem here extends to other areas of life too. The fact is that you like variety in everything and so can tire of situations that fail to offer it. All the same, if you choose wisely and learn to understand your restless side, then great happiness can be yours.

47

Venus in Capricorn

The most notable trait that comes from Venus in this position is that it makes you trustworthy and able to take on all sorts of responsibilities in life. People are instinctively fond of you and love you all the more because you are always ready to help those who are in any form of need. Social and business popularity can be yours and there is a magnetic quality to your nature that is particularly attractive in a romantic sense. Anyone who wants a partner for a lover, a spouse and a good friend too would almost certainly look in your direction. Constancy is the hallmark of your nature and unfaithfulness would go right against the grain. You might sometimes be a little too trusting.

Venus in Aquarius

This location of Venus offers a fondness for travel and a desire to try out something new at every possible opportunity. You are extremely easy to get along with and tend to have many friends from varied backgrounds, classes and inclinations. You like to live a distinct sort of life and gain a great deal from moving about, both in a career sense and with regard to your home. It is not out of the question that you could form a romantic attachment to someone who comes from far away or be attracted to a person of a distinctly artistic and original nature. What you cannot stand is jealousy, for you have friends of both sexes and would want to keep things that way.

Venus in Pisces

The first thing people tend to notice about you is your wonderful, warm smile. Being very charitable by nature you will do anything to help others, even if you don't know them well. Much of your life may be spent sorting out situations for other people, but it is very important to feel that you are living for yourself too. In the main, you remain cheerful, and tend to be quite attractive to members of the opposite sex. Where romantic attachments are concerned, you could be drawn to people who are significantly older or younger than yourself or to someone with a unique career or point of view. It might be best for you to avoid marrying whilst you are still very young.

AQUARIUS:
2014 DIARY PAGES

October 2014

1 WEDNESDAY   *Moon Age Day 7   Moon Sign Sagittarius*

Any Aquarians who may have been feeling slightly out of sorts across the last few days may now find that they feel a good deal better. There is certainly likely to be a more positive attitude coming in from the world at large and some of those things you have wanted to do for a while but were restricted from completing are now possible.

2 THURSDAY   *Moon Age Day 8   Moon Sign Capricorn*

You are intriguing and intrigued today – it's a two-way process. Almost anything can captivate your curiosity and imagination and at the same time people are looking at you with a sense of fascination. What are you doing to engender these strange reactions? Nothing at all except being a fairly typical Aquarian subject.

3 FRIDAY   *Moon Age Day 9   Moon Sign Capricorn*

You benefit from being on the move under present planetary trends and might not be too satisfied with life if you have to stay put or tend to ordinary routines. If you do have heavy responsibilities, try to delegate – at least for today. Even a few hours away from everyday cares can prove to be very important.

4 SATURDAY   *Moon Age Day 10   Moon Sign Aquarius*

You should focus on being on target as far as your goals and ambitions are concerned. You can afford to put a great deal of faith in your natural luck for today and tomorrow and will have what it takes to get ahead of the crowd, either at work or socially. What really sees you winning out is your natural optimism.

5 SUNDAY
☿ *Moon Age Day 11   Moon Sign Aquarius*

This is another red-letter day for most Aquarians and a time when you are clearly firing on all cylinders. Whilst others fall by the wayside regarding new plans and altered situations, you show yourself to be flexible and happy to co-operate. All of this gets you noticed in a big way and ensures you are stocking up potential gains for later.

6 MONDAY
☿   *Moon Age Day 12   Moon Sign Pisces*

This could turn out to be one of the most progressive Mondays you will experience during the autumn. You have a greater than average capacity to keep going, well after others have fallen by the wayside. There are advantages coming your way that you may not have previously expected but the important thing is that you react quickly.

7 TUESDAY
☿   *Moon Age Day 13   Moon Sign Pisces*

The general state of romance improves under present planetary trends and that means today could find you in wonderful company and saying exactly the right things to deepen an existing attachment or to form one in the first place. You are rarely stuck for words but just at present they drip from your tongue like honey.

8 WEDNESDAY
☿   *Moon Age Day 14   Moon Sign Aries*

There are times when a tried-and-tested approach is the best one to adopt, though you rarely seem to realise the fact. Everything in your life is change and originality – that's just the way you are. Nevertheless if you don't follow an expected path today you could be brought firmly down to earth with a bump before evening.

9 THURSDAY
☿   *Moon Age Day 15   Moon Sign Aries*

Whilst others get all complicated about solving little problems, you can have them sorted in no time at all. This is the sort of behaviour that gets you noticed and especially so under present planetary trends. You barely have to open your mouth today before someone declares you to be a genius. It might not be true but it is gratifying.

10 FRIDAY ☿ *Moon Age Day 16* *Moon Sign Taurus*

Most noteworthy of all in your life just now is likely to be your creative potential. You will know instinctively what looks and feels right and can really wow people with your sense of style. Add to this a very positive attitude to life and an expression that says you can't believe everyone is not as cool as you are and success will follow.

11 SATURDAY ☿ *Moon Age Day 17* *Moon Sign Taurus*

Despite your constant need to alter anything and everything at the drop of a hat it is the stable work patterns and normal actions that bring the greatest potential rewards for the moment. Still that butterfly mind and leave some of your originality alone, at least during this weekend. Someone you know well has a very good idea today.

12 SUNDAY ☿ *Moon Age Day 18* *Moon Sign Gemini*

Progress could be significantly slowed at this stage of the weekend but more because of the actions of other people than on account of anything you are saying or doing. All you can really do is to show a degree of patience and to help out whenever it proves to be possible. Fortunately your social life is anything but slow.

13 MONDAY ☿ *Moon Age Day 19* *Moon Sign Gemini*

You now show a strong desire to agree with others and to find a way forward, even where there have been significant difficulties in the past. You should also find that you are particularly good at pouring oil on troubled waters as far as friends are concerned and should play the honest broker more than once as this week gets into gear.

14 TUESDAY ☿ *Moon Age Day 20* *Moon Sign Cancer*

Confidence is clearly present, even if it sometimes feels as though you are walking a tightrope today. Above all, you can afford to be quite courageous at the moment and could find yourself confidently facing people and situations that have unnerved you in the past. Even if you quake inside, just keep that to yourself.

15 WEDNESDAY ☿   *Moon Age Day 21*   *Moon Sign Cancer*

There is now a chance that you could be faced with an opportunity to bring in more money over the next few weeks. Part of you says that you are involved in pipe dreams whilst your deeper reasoning tells you to go ahead. There is no harm in at least exploring these avenues – that is if you are observant enough to recognise them.

16 THURSDAY ☿   *Moon Age Day 22*   *Moon Sign Cancer*

The emphasis at the moment is on the practical side of life. You may not have as much time for personal enjoyment as you might wish but the important thing is that you are getting things done and that will please you in the longer term. Career developments should be going your way at this time.

17 FRIDAY ☿   *Moon Age Day 23*   *Moon Sign Leo*

Certain aspects of material progress could be difficult whilst the lunar low is around. You may be feeling less than your usual confident self and not quite so inclined to speak out in company. This would be a good time to spend as much time as possible on your own.

18 SATURDAY ☿   *Moon Age Day 24*   *Moon Sign Leo*

Patience could be tested by life's little drawbacks but there is enough planetary support around you now for you to get through or round problems. It's simply that you are not on top form and so taking unnecessary risks is probably not to be recommended. Routines will seem comfortable and you need security now.

19 SUNDAY ☿   *Moon Age Day 25*   *Moon Sign Virgo*

The emphasis is on fun and on you being able to show others that you are willing to join in and be part of the group. There are times when Aquarius is more than happy to watch and wait but October simply isn't like that for you. On the contrary, whatever is happening around you – chances are you are inspiring it.

20 MONDAY ☿ *Moon Age Day 26* *Moon Sign Virgo*

A rather busy phase is likely at work, but you are not really up for the challenge today. This is a situation that will change soon enough but for today you need to feel comfortable so avoid risk-taking. If you are feeling a little insecure, turn to your partner and family members for support.

21 TUESDAY ☿ *Moon Age Day 27* *Moon Sign Virgo*

Better fortune and plain good luck should follow you around now. It will be easy for you to make the right sort of decisions and you will be less inclined than ever to hang back when there are gains to be made. On the romantic front, the trends offer you an especially good interlude across the coming days.

22 WEDNESDAY ☿ *Moon Age Day 28* *Moon Sign Libra*

Avoid domestic dealings as they may prove to be somewhat tense and tempers could fray. It might appear as if others are at fault but that probably isn't the case. It takes two to tango so if you refuse to get involved in the dispute, then it will not materialise. However, that might not be too easy when you feel you are being severely provoked.

23 THURSDAY ☿ *Moon Age Day 0* *Moon Sign Libra*

A money matter needs a more cautious approach and you may be feeling less keen to part with cash than was sometimes the case earlier in October. Watch out for casual acquaintances who could become much more to you in the days ahead. Try to take a fresh perspective on old situations before today is out.

24 FRIDAY ☿ *Moon Age Day 1* *Moon Sign Scorpio*

Discussing practical matters with others is the best way to stir up some ingenious ideas today. You tend to be quite discriminating and won't settle for second best in anything. Not everyone will follow your lead at this time but the people who matter the most to you should be falling in line and conspire to make you feel quite important.

25 SATURDAY ☿ *Moon Age Day 2   Moon Sign Scorpio*

There are exciting possibilities in the offing. If you work at the weekend it is likely to be your career that offers new advantages but if the day is your own, turn your energy towards having fun. Either way you continue to give every evidence of knowing what you are doing and of being extremely capable.

26 SUNDAY *Moon Age Day 3   Moon Sign Scorpio*

The practicalities of life are inclined to take up most of your time but you may hear something to your advantage if you make sure you are listening. There could be a strong feeling that important times are at hand so you need to be very discriminating when it comes to long-term plans or commitments.

27 MONDAY *Moon Age Day 4   Moon Sign Sagittarius*

You have a good feel for group activities at the moment so be ready to co-operate with anyone who seems to have similar ideas and intentions to your own. A lighter and zanier side begins to show itself to some Aquarians and you could even surprise yourself with a tendency to do things that attract an audience.

28 TUESDAY *Moon Age Day 5   Moon Sign Sagittarius*

Your social life can be quite inspiring and it looks as though you will be keen to enlist the support of others and advance your goals through partnerships of one sort or another. There is plenty to be done at the moment but such is your attitude and your resilience that most jobs are undertaken in half the time you would normally expect.

29 WEDNESDAY *Moon Age Day 6   Moon Sign Capricorn*

Acts of common kindness and friendliness on your part are not unusual but there are more of them about right now. That's because your empathy is strong and you should use those influences to good effect. Almost anyone is likely to turn to you for support or advice and you should ensure they are not disappointed.

30 THURSDAY   *Moon Age Day 7   Moon Sign Capricorn*

Whilst you are now able to communicate and to put forward your point of view in an almost forthright manner, not everyone is going to respond positively to what you have to say. Be careful that you strike a balance and do not come across as being over-assertive or even dominant. More sharing is necessary because that brings bigger dividends.

31 FRIDAY   *Moon Age Day 8   Moon Sign Aquarius*

The lunar high brings a strong end to the month and will almost certainly surround you with a greater sense of freedom to make your own choices for success. It isn't as if money is being handed to you in buckets but you do now have a greater sense of purpose so use it to sniff out some genuine advantages.

November 2014

1 SATURDAY
Moon Age Day 9   Moon Sign Aquarius

Don't be afraid to take the odd gamble because you are extremely astute and capable at the moment. This is no time for standing in the shadows but rather the moment when you should put yourself out there in the mainstream of life. Aquarius can be very unconventional now but that's how you enjoy being.

2 SUNDAY
Moon Age Day 10   Moon Sign Pisces

You should find that any problems that do come along will be short-lived and fairly manageable. Take some time out to enjoy yourself today. All too soon the dark days of winter will be here and you may wish then that you had seen more of the world beyond your own door. A long walk in beautiful surroundings would set you up wonderfully for a new week.

3 MONDAY
Moon Age Day 11   Moon Sign Pisces

You should be on a roll at work. Issues here bring valuable highlights and your inventive mind will be constantly on the go. There is a sideways look at personal securities around this time but this tendency won't prevent you from taking the odd chance or for pushing your luck in your contacts with bosses.

4 TUESDAY
Moon Age Day 12   Moon Sign Aries

There is a chance that more money could be coming your way during this week but only if you pay attention and get things right first time. It is also likely that you will benefit from efforts you put in previously and as a result of opportunities you may have thought were lost and gone forever.

5 WEDNESDAY
Moon Age Day 13   Moon Sign Aries

There is potential today for you to put yourself at the disposal of others, both inside and outside of work. Some Aquarians will now be thinking in terms of new interests or hobbies and if you are one of them it is important to move away from the pedestrian and the normal towards something truly expressive.

6 THURSDAY
Moon Age Day 14   Moon Sign Taurus

It is towards your home life that you are most likely to be looking today and maybe until the coming weekend. Relatives may be especially kind to you right now and, suspicious as you are under present planetary trends, you might wonder just what it is they are after. You are about to find out!

7 FRIDAY
Moon Age Day 15   Moon Sign Taurus

It looks as though for a day or two at least you will be dispensing with your usual idealism in favour of practical common sense. That works well in most cases but be aware that people who like and trust your nature might feel you have suddenly become much more cynical than usual. Remember the adage 'moderation in all things'.

8 SATURDAY
Moon Age Day 16   Moon Sign Taurus

You are likely to be on good form so remember to remain open to new suggestions and all manner of possibilities. If you are an Aquarian who does not work at the weekend, it might be good if you earmark a good part of today to do something radically different. Invitations tend to come from friends and you are less likely to stick around home just now.

9 SUNDAY
Moon Age Day 17   Moon Sign Gemini

When it comes to getting your own way, use all the weapons in your personal armoury today. Number one is your wonderful nature, which exudes joy and encourages others at every turn. In addition you are quite persuasive now and have what it takes to convince everyone that what you want is also their ideal.

10 MONDAY   *Moon Age Day 18   Moon Sign Gemini*

Today you show yourself to be very assertive and certainly won't take no for an answer with regard to anything you see as being important. Neither will you be in the market for an argument because you can stamp on anyone's opposition long before it gets to any sort of fallout.

11 TUESDAY   *Moon Age Day 19   Moon Sign Cancer*

Chances are that you are gradually growing more reasonable, which is good because you will be less inclined to force your ideas on to others. This has been a strange departure for you because although Aquarius is a great thinker and even an intellectual, it isn't normally your way to dominate situations or people. An apology might just be called for.

12 WEDNESDAY   *Moon Age Day 20   Moon Sign Cancer*

There isn't any doubt at present about how attractive you are to others. This is likely to be made so plain it could lead to the odd embarrassing situation, especially since you can be quite naïve on occasions. What you take for natural kindness and someone's warm disposition could turn out to be much more.

13 THURSDAY   *Moon Age Day 21   Moon Sign Leo*

The lunar low might slow you down a little but you can make sure it doesn't prevent the general momentum you have built up in your life as a whole. Don't let anyone lord it over you at present and be prepared to stick up for yourself, even when you are not absolutely sure of your ground. Support from others comes later.

14 FRIDAY   *Moon Age Day 22   Moon Sign Leo*

Your mental prowess deepens and when it comes to thinking things through nobody could beat you today. Anything really odd will capture your interest and you may also show a great fondness for history or culture around this time. The people who surround you see you as being particularly intelligent – which only goes to show how perceptive they are!

15 SATURDAY   *Moon Age Day 23   Moon Sign Leo*

Look out for those mechanical and electrical devices, all of which may seem to have a down on you today. It might be best not to interfere too much and to allow people who know what they doing to sort things out. Meanwhile put your mind to newer and better ways to spoil your friends and to motivate your relatives.

16 SUNDAY   *Moon Age Day 24   Moon Sign Virgo*

Because you are so good to have around, you are likely to be in great demand at the moment. This isn't just a social thing but most likely extends to other spheres of your life too. When it comes to making a decision that is going to have a bearing on where you will be around this time next year, you may need to make your mind up now.

17 MONDAY   *Moon Age Day 25   Moon Sign Virgo*

This is one of the best times of the month to reach out and make contacts far beyond the scope of your usual circle. Maybe you are busy on the internet, speaking to people who live far away, or it could simply be that your work has a long-distance aspect now. Any form of travel would suit you down to the ground and change is vital.

18 TUESDAY   *Moon Age Day 26   Moon Sign Libra*

Channel some of your present energies into changes you want to make in and around your home. You could be putting some sort of pressure on your own personal life, maybe because you are less willing than usual to compromise over issues that really are not that important. Give and take is essential if you are to really enjoy today.

19 WEDNESDAY   *Moon Age Day 27   Moon Sign Libra*

The focus for the moment is on exploring and enlarging your personal creativity. Getting things looking good is very important to you at the best of times but especially so just now. You will also be inclined to show off more in a romantic sense so make sure you are looking your best.

20 THURSDAY   *Moon Age Day 28   Moon Sign Libra*

This would be the best time of the month to start a new romantic relationship, though of course if you are settled enough with your present partner that isn't going to be an option. All the same, there is nothing to prevent you from bringing a little more pep into your love life. Aquarius has a good and active imagination so use it now.

21 FRIDAY   *Moon Age Day 29   Moon Sign Scorpio*

The influences suggest that your dealings with others might lead to a few pleasant encounters and could even be responsible for a friendship that will endure for life. The vibes are good for your love life, too, so use the prevailing energies to sweep someone special off their feet. Avoid unnecessary and tedious chores today.

22 SATURDAY   *Moon Age Day 0   Moon Sign Scorpio*

Stay close to loved ones today as your emotional responses will be deeper and ever more tangible to those you care for. Expressing the way you feel isn't always that easy but you should take advantage of the fact that it will seem easier now. As a result you are likely to be on the receiving end of equally truthful admissions.

23 SUNDAY   *Moon Age Day 1   Moon Sign Sagittarius*

With a little effort on your part it is clear that old situations will be fading away and that you can put your mind to what is both new and exciting. Putting the finishing touches to something that has taken you ages could put you in an even better frame of mind and you are also likely to be extremely generous in your dealings with others.

24 MONDAY   *Moon Age Day 2   Moon Sign Sagittarius*

Right now you seem to have the secret of popularity and that is worth a great deal in terms of how well you get on generally. This would be an excellent time to be out socialising but you should also be getting on very well at work. You should find this to be an excellent way to start the new working week and there are plenty of gains to be made.

25 TUESDAY   *Moon Age Day 3   Moon Sign Capricorn*

It looks as though you will be quite happy to take the lead this week so start today as you mean to go on. That means a sudden and somewhat unexpected rush of energy that could leave others puzzled and dizzy. It might be best to explain yourself before you begin the whirlwind. That way people are in the picture.

26 WEDNESDAY   *Moon Age Day 4   Moon Sign Capricorn*

You want to reshape things and if you set out with determination you could even surprise yourself. Not everyone is going to be on your side today but when the chips are down you will learn quickly enough who your best supporters are. Don't be too quick to dismiss an idea that might turn out to be a crackerjack in the end.

27 THURSDAY   *Moon Age Day 5   Moon Sign Aquarius*

Things can go from fairly quiet to positively hectic today so keep your wits about you so you can benefit from everything that is on offer. Only an Aquarian would try to do so, but things look so inviting you probably can't help yourself. Romance is especially well highlighted today with new understandings developing for some.

28 FRIDAY   *Moon Age Day 6   Moon Sign Aquarius*

This is a marvellous time in which to be assertive and to make your feelings known. So powerful is your personality at present it is very unlikely you would be refused any reasonable request. Getting what you want from life is only half the picture because you are also doing everything you can to make those around you happy too.

29 SATURDAY   *Moon Age Day 7   Moon Sign Pisces*

Saturday might seem positively pedestrian after the last few days but in reality you are able to achieve a great deal, so remain cheerful in the way you go about it. There is a good chance that family members and also close friends are very approachable at this time and you will enjoy your interactions with them.

30 SUNDAY
Moon Age Day 8   Moon Sign Pisces

Material matters are now going very much your way and the day favours you from the start, so make sure you fit in as much as you can. If you apply an increased sense of purpose, you could look out for financial gains from your own efforts or a partner's. If you use your skills, everything will fall into place when you need it the most.

December
2014

1 MONDAY
Moon Age Day 9   Moon Sign Pisces

It's up to you today to put in that extra bit of effort that can really make a difference. The planets say right now that if you leave things alone, that's the way they will stay, whereas if you interfere with life a little, almost anything is possible. Don't allow anyone to push you to the back of the queue today, either at work or socially.

2 TUESDAY
Moon Age Day 10   Moon Sign Aries

Not everyone is going to agree with you today, particularly in a domestic sense. That's why you will have to make some compromises at home this week. It might be a simple disagreement over which television channel to watch or something more serious but there doesn't need to be any bother at all if you make sure you are fair.

3 WEDNESDAY
Moon Age Day 11   Moon Sign Aries

If you want to make things happen in a practical sense, this is the part of the month to get moving. There can be significant changes at work for some, whilst other Aquarians will be making changes to their social lives. In many respects it's off with the old and on with the new – which is always of interest to your zodiac sign.

4 THURSDAY
Moon Age Day 12   Moon Sign Taurus

This great balance between your outward-facing self and your inward-looking qualities continues today – and will be stable as long as you think and act in a positive and yet thoughtful manner. It seems as though practically everyone likes you at the moment, though of course there are bound to be exceptions.

5 FRIDAY
Moon Age Day 13   Moon Sign Taurus

Being an Aquarian and therefore always busy, it might only now have occurred to you that Christmas is just around the corner. That means you are going to have to get cracking right away because there are lots of things that need organising and maybe all those presents to buy. Put in some effort and there will be no need to panic just yet.

6 SATURDAY
Moon Age Day 14   Moon Sign Gemini

Standing up for yourself is no problem now, though there could be occasions when you are inclined to defend yourself before you are attacked. This may not turn out to be the best family Saturday of the month, partly because everyone seems to have different ideas and won't listen to yours – which, of course, are the best of all!

7 SUNDAY
Moon Age Day 15   Moon Sign Gemini

You can certainly get frustrated at the moment if you sense that limitations are being placed upon you and that is likely to cause you to react. In discussions, you could be slightly prickly but in the main you manage to understand that not everyone thinks the same. If anything really annoys you today it is likely to be people who are selfish.

8 MONDAY
Moon Age Day 16   Moon Sign Cancer

Your current best course of action is to continue to be light-hearted and happy to fall in line with what your friends and especially your partner want to do. There is a strong sense of curiosity about you at the moment so indulge it by looking into not only what happens but why, which might mean a bit of digging. Your love life should be comfortable.

9 TUESDAY
Moon Age Day 17   Moon Sign Cancer

There ought to be plenty of support about but you are showing a great deal of care and concern for others yourself. Look towards a warm and considerate sort of day all round, with some special highlights later on. People who are living abroad or who you see very rarely could be getting in touch with you at any time now.

10 WEDNESDAY *Moon Age Day 18   Moon Sign Cancer*

It may be more difficult than normal to explain yourself to others but if you make the effort it will be worth it because you will only get the support and help you need when other people are conversant with your thinking. Don't rush your fences but take time out to weigh up the pros and cons of any situation.

11 THURSDAY *Moon Age Day 19   Moon Sign Leo*

It would be a very good idea to take a more relaxed attitude and to watch and wait. Although the lunar low is not very potent this month, it can cause you to make silly mistakes if you expect to carry on at your usual speed. Instead of making all the decisions yourself right now, you should defer to family members and friends.

12 FRIDAY *Moon Age Day 20   Moon Sign Leo*

This is a day for making the most of sudden possibilities that come along. Don't be stubborn or stick to what you always do – take a chance and act quickly and decisively. With more luck now attending your actions, you have what it takes to get ahead and can invent new ways of dealing with tedious routines. Friends are supportive now.

13 SATURDAY *Moon Age Day 21   Moon Sign Virgo*

Today you need change and diversity and no matter how much family members demand your attention, you would be better off seeking the company of friends at some stage. The trouble is that you remain active and enterprising but have little or no way to utilise this side of your nature under present trends.

14 SUNDAY *Moon Age Day 22   Moon Sign Virgo*

You should be feeling slightly more relaxed today and more willing to go with the flow than seems to have been the case across the last few days. Relatives may make demands of you, even if it is only that they think you are a free taxi service. However, on the whole you stand a good chance of enjoying today.

15 MONDAY   *Moon Age Day 23   Moon Sign Virgo*

If there is one thing you relish at the moment it's a challenge. You are certainly not likely to shy away from any opportunity to pit your wits against people you respect as being good competitors and you are especially fair in your attitude right now. Keep your ears open because even a casual conversation could carry important messages.

16 TUESDAY   *Moon Age Day 24   Moon Sign Libra*

Right now you are the sort of person that others notice and that means being put in the spotlight – even when you would prefer not to be. If nothing else, soak up the attention as it will do your ego a power of good, and trust other people's good opinion as it is well placed. Concentration is vital at work.

17 WEDNESDAY   *Moon Age Day 25   Moon Sign Libra*

Getting ahead would be difficult today, which is why, if you are wise, you won't bother trying. Instead of knocking your head against a brick wall you would be better watching and waiting for a couple of days. For Aquarians who are not at work today there should be a chance to put your feet up and to let others take the strain.

18 THURSDAY   *Moon Age Day 26   Moon Sign Scorpio*

You will want things on course when it comes to practical matters and all arrangements. It is a good time to get in touch with powerful emotions at the moment and to confront issues you have been putting to the back of your mind in recent days. In social settings, your ability to make people laugh will stand you in good stead.

19 FRIDAY   *Moon Age Day 27   Moon Sign Scorpio*

This is almost certainly a day to opt for wide-open spaces and for alterations in your daily routines. Comfort and security take something of a back seat as you set out to explore the world with eyes wide open and a sense of wonder in your heart. Bringing yourself back to the essentials of life won't be easy at any time today.

20 SATURDAY *Moon Age Day 28   Moon Sign Sagittarius*

Close twosomes have a positive part to play at the moment so use your ability to find just the right words to make your partner feel wanted and secure. The same is true in reverse because expressions of love bring a sense of warmth into your day and make it rather special. Don't get too tied down with pointless routines just now.

21 SUNDAY *Moon Age Day 29   Moon Sign Sagittarius*

It seems as though you will get on better today if you do your own thing, rather than catering for everyone else. That doesn't mean you are being selfish. Not everyone has your staying power or your ability to work quickly through potential problems. By tomorrow you should be feeling more settled and secure.

22 MONDAY *Moon Age Day 0   Moon Sign Sagittarius*

Only a few days to go to Christmas and it is likely that you are way behind with your final preparations. Does this really worry you? Things will happen whether you monitor them or not and everyone will manage to have a good time, even without each little detail being perfect. It's time for Aquarius to relax; you just don't realise it yet.

23 TUESDAY *Moon Age Day 1   Moon Sign Capricorn*

A romance or love affair at this time could prove to be all-consuming and people you meet at the moment will have a lasting emotional impact on your life. Some jobs today can seem to take twice as long as usual but that is probably because you insist on getting every nuance and detail right. Don't worry if others laugh at your attitude.

24 WEDNESDAY *Moon Age Day 2   Moon Sign Capricorn*

This is likely to be a potentially good Christmas Eve for love, though more of the dreamy, poetical sort than the forceful, caveman type. In some respects you might be just a little quiet but sandwiched between some strong planetary aspects and the arrival of the Moon into the sign of Aquarius, that isn't going to last for very long.

25 THURSDAY   *Moon Age Day 3   Moon Sign Aquarius*

Things should be going your way for Christmas Day and you won't want to slow life down at all. Not everyone has your staying power so there are occasions when it will be necessary to go it alone but even this is no real problem just now. You can afford to push your luck a little, but despite the Moon's position this is not a time for overt gambling.

26 FRIDAY   *Moon Age Day 4   Moon Sign Aquarius*

You will be feeling now as if you want to overdo everything and to live your life in a grand style. People generally will be accommodating and will join in with your ideas. The need for luxury is strong so grasp any opportunity to spoil yourself firmly with both hands. Use your creative potential now.

27 SATURDAY   *Moon Age Day 5   Moon Sign Pisces*

Tensions at home can come from trying to get too much done in too short a period of time. Try not to worry too much about insignificant social details. Things that don't get sorted out to your exacting standards will still come and go and then you will wonder why you worried at all.

28 SUNDAY   *Moon Age Day 6   Moon Sign Pisces*

There is no lack of things to do at this stage of the week and you could just feel that the right sort of support from those around you isn't always forthcoming. If you feel inclined to be rather more outspoken than might sometimes be the case, think before you speak or risk upsetting someone more timid than you.

29 MONDAY   *Moon Age Day 7   Moon Sign Aries*

Getting out and about is the best choice if you want to be mentally and physically stimulated. You love to meet new people and you should take the time to observe things you haven't noticed before – even if they are only a stone's throw from your own home! Take advantage of great social and romantic influences.

30 TUESDAY   *Moon Age Day 8   Moon Sign Aries*

You can expand your experience base today by doing something completely different. After all, a new year lies just around the corner and that's a time when alternative experiences are most opportune. Some of you may be feeling as if the time is right to get back to normal life but for the next day or two you need to curb your impatience.

31 WEDNESDAY   *Moon Age Day 9   Moon Sign Taurus*

There are some good planetary trends around today and these ensure that the last day of the year is likely to go extremely well for you. Once again, you will be happy to stand out in a crowd and should be the life and soul of any New Year party you decide to attend. What a great way to finish 2014 and to start 2015!

AQUARIUS:
2015 DIARY PAGES

AQUARIUS:
YOUR YEAR IN BRIEF

Aquarius enjoys the cut and thrust that comes with each new January. As the year dawns you will be itching to get going, and January and February offer you the perfect circumstances for making progress. You don't mind the winter weather too much and you will be making great strides in terms of career and with regard to relationships. Money matters will be variable but improving and there are gains to be made from long-term plans.

March and April should bring you to a better understanding of what is necessary if you want to make real advancements in your life this year. As time goes by you should have greater confidence and will be receiving more tangible support from people who are in the best position to offer it. Money matters should be stronger and there is a good chance that you will be travelling more throughout this period. A trip across the water isn't out of the question during April.

May and June look like being very fortunate months, and as the weather improves and the lighter nights are in evidence you will be filling your days with new potentials, and probably also spending much more time out of doors amongst people you recognise as being adventurous and exciting. This is not a time for you to hide your light under a bushel and you need to let the world know you are around.

July and August are months of change and diversity for you. Almost anything can be turned on its head, though always in a positive way. In a professional sense, you could be thinking about changing your job and you will also be keen to seek out fresh fields and pastures new as much as proves to be possible. In fact, very little is impossible for you at this time and you show how positive you can be.

September and October work out well for you. This is definitely a good time for you and a period when you show yourself to the world at your best. Don't get tied down with too much red tape and try to stay flexible in all your dealings. Romance looks good, but you are likely to be busy in all spheres of your life and you come across as being an innovator and someone with great charisma.

November and December have their own particular magic. This is partly because of your gentler and less hurried attitude and the amount of time you are willing to give to your lover, relatives and friends. Acquaintances can become much more in the approach to the Christmas period and you should be in the market for a happy family time during which you take the lead in social events. End the year on a decisive note by announcing a major change for 2016.

January
2015

1 THURSDAY
Moon Age Day 11 Moon Sign Taurus

This could be a good start to the year for you. Quickly leaving behind all the festivities, you will almost immediately be in a practical frame of mind and anxious to get ahead. The enforced rest will have refreshed you and given your fertile mind a chance to look at new possibilities.

2 FRIDAY
Moon Age Day 12 Moon Sign Gemini

It seems as though much of your attention will now be focused on loved ones and the very real demands they seem to place on you. Younger people especially would gain from your experience and advice, even though you won't want to be forcing yourself upon them. Make a very tactful approach, as only you can.

3 SATURDAY
Moon Age Day 13 Moon Sign Gemini

Freedom is the key today and you have a burning desire to do what appeals to you at any point in time. Some frustration could therefore occur on those occasions when you are tied down by circumstances and conventions. Don't be too quick to jump into an argument at work. Let things stew for a while.

4 SUNDAY
Moon Age Day 14 Moon Sign Gemini

Someone you haven't seen for ages could be making a return visit to your life this Sunday, or perhaps you are being inundated with text messages or emails from people you don't contact too often. All of this forces your mind into the past, but you should not allow this to get in the way of progress now.

5 MONDAY
Moon Age Day 15 Moon Sign Cancer

It looks as though social arrangements of one sort or another will keep a smile on your face at present. The first day of the working week for many of you offers newer and better incentives to get ahead, even if there are one or two people around at the moment who don't seem to have your best interests at heart.

6 TUESDAY
Moon Age Day 16 Moon Sign Cancer

Avoid rising to the bait if you feel you are being goaded right now. Of course it is important to stand up for yourself, but there are times when you appear to be defending yourself before you have even been attacked. Keep busy and stay as physically active as circumstances allow.

7 WEDNESDAY
Moon Age Day 17 Moon Sign Leo

There might be some conflict around today, either at work or at home. You can put this down to the position of the Moon, which moves into your opposite zodiac sign of Leo today. This represents that period of the month that is known as the lunar low, a time when you need to be just a little more careful.

8 THURSDAY
Moon Age Day 18 Moon Sign Leo

Getting on with things is harder right now and demands more of your time and effort. Actually, you might decide that the struggle really isn't worthwhile and that you would be better off watching and waiting until tomorrow at least. Friends will remain helpful and can take some of the weight off your shoulders.

9 FRIDAY
Moon Age Day 19 Moon Sign Virgo

Rather than being strictly physical today, you opt for a more thoughtful approach. You prove to be diplomatic, which is quite typical of your zodiac sign, and can easily play the honest broker when friends fail to see eye to eye. People from the past are once again inclined to pay a return visit to your life around now.

10 SATURDAY   *Moon Age Day 20 Moon Sign Virgo*

Your winning ways are certainly on display and you can get most of what you want by showing a little of that Aquarian cheek and by being willing to ask. Even in situations that could have worried you in the past, you show greater reserves of courage, together with the Air-sign magic that is your astrological legacy.

11 SUNDAY   *Moon Age Day 21 Moon Sign Virgo*

Change and growth are inevitable facts of life under present trends and you need to be sure that you are not sticking to a particular way of thinking just because it is more comfortable to do so. In any case, life itself tends to give you a slight kick up the rear around now, but it should prove to be very positive in the end.

12 MONDAY   *Moon Age Day 22 Moon Sign Libra*

With everything to play for, you are approaching new matters with the level of optimism that typifies your zodiac sign when working at its best. New incentives at work could find you taking on newer and better responsibilities, and you attract all manner of people by simply being yourself.

13 TUESDAY   *Moon Age Day 23 Moon Sign Libra*

Getting on with whatever demands your attention is easy for now, even though you could feel on occasions that you are carrying burdens that don't rightfully belong to you. In a family sense, it is important to allow younger people especially to have their head and to make up their own minds about life.

14 WEDNESDAY   *Moon Age Day 24 Moon Sign Scorpio*

Friends and associates are likely to show you their support, sometimes in a very practical way and you won't have much difficulty in getting your message across when it counts the most. Romance continues to play an important part in your thinking and at work you may be soaking up new responsibilities.

15 THURSDAY   *Moon Age Day 25 Moon Sign Scorpio*

Socially speaking you are likely to be on top of the world. Pushing yourself too hard at work would be a waste of time, because you get most of what you want by simply turning on the charm. When friends argue, you once again show yourself to be a genuine honest broker and as a result they trust you.

16 FRIDAY   *Moon Age Day 26 Moon Sign Scorpio*

Others are inclined to listen to what you have to say, so this is clearly a time to say what you think. Whether you will be quite as tactful as you should be today remains to be seen, but you do have some diplomacy to call upon if you keep the feelings of others in mind. Attitude is very important at work.

17 SATURDAY   *Moon Age Day 27 Moon Sign Sagittarius*

You will be able to get the best from social situations today and show the very gregarious side of your Aquarian nature. Not everyone you meet will be equally helpful, but you do have what to takes to talk awkward types round to your point of view. Your charming persona remains intact.

18 SUNDAY   *Moon Age Day 28 Moon Sign Sagittarius*

This is likely to be an inspiring sort of day and one during which you are able to get masses done. Once again, much relies on your ability to communicate and you have what it takes to turn heads when it really matters. Keep an eye out for small financial gains and plans for others in the near future.

19 MONDAY   *Moon Age Day 29 Moon Sign Capricorn*

Don't be afraid to take the odd chance today, especially at work. You are capable and have great determination, something that others are almost certain to recognise. Action is the name of the game and you won't take no for an answer in situations you understand well. You should be physically restless today.

20 TUESDAY · *Moon Age Day 0 · Moon Sign Capricorn*

Those around you now seem to be in a good position to offer you both help and advice. What is less certain is whether you are willing to listen. Aquarius is quieter than usual, thanks to a twelfth house Moon, but you will have patience and persistence enough to achieve an objective that has been around for a while.

21 WEDNESDAY · *Moon Age Day 1 · Moon Sign Aquarius*

Along comes that special time of the month during which the Moon occupies your own zodiac sign of Aquarius. This two or three-day period is known as the lunar high and is a time during which you are filled with new incentives and energy. Luck tends to be on your side and you are more likely to take a chance.

22 THURSDAY ☿ · *Moon Age Day 2 · Moon Sign Aquarius*

The green light is still on. This is a time during which you need to create room for yourself and a period when you can afford to act with greater determination. Few of your objectives seem impossible and you continue to seek your own fortune, as well as charming just about everyone you meet on the way.

23 FRIDAY ☿ · *Moon Age Day 3 · Moon Sign Pisces*

Friendship issues and group encounters take up much of your time and you are likely to be quite gregarious in a social sense. You won't want to spend much time concentrating on practical issues and the very best scenario would be to spend time away from home and doing something exciting.

24 SATURDAY ☿ · *Moon Age Day 4 · Moon Sign Pisces*

Although confidence is likely to be high and you are getting a great deal done, you might be fretting over money. Look at the situation carefully and you should discover that things are nowhere near as sticky as you may have feared. Get on side with colleagues who you also count as good friends.

25 SUNDAY ☿ *Moon Age Day 5 Moon Sign Aries*

There are likely to be some positive highlights related to family matters and you have what it takes to move mountains for others. This means there will probably be less time to address issues that are important to you personally, but you are very practically minded and will be able to think up new schemes as you go along.

26 MONDAY ☿ *Moon Age Day 6 Moon Sign Aries*

Look out for new information that comes in at the start of a new working week. People are likely to rely heavily on you, but you will be fine when put under any sort of pressure. The attitude of a loved one might take some thinking about and some effort is necessary when it comes to remaining calm in the face of provocation.

27 TUESDAY ☿ *Moon Age Day 7 Moon Sign Taurus*

Better financial developments could easily be on the way, even if some of them are a little difficult to spot right now. Creative potential is also good and there is a strong chance that you are finding things to do around the house that will make both you and other family members more comfortable in the longer term.

28 WEDNESDAY ☿ *Moon Age Day 8 Moon Sign Taurus*

You should be well organised today, which is just as well because you are likely to be quite busy and not able to give as much attention to certain matters as you might wish. Don't get involved in disputes that have nothing at all to do with you and settle for a quieter day in terms of your interactions with others.

29 THURSDAY ☿ *Moon Age Day 9 Moon Sign Gemini*

Keep an eye out for some unexpected successes. These are not likely to be regarding major issues and you will also find that you are winding down somewhat later on. By the evening, you will probably be very happy to watch and wait, rather than taking part.

30 FRIDAY ☿ *Moon Age Day 10 Moon Sign Gemini*

Recent efforts begin to show positive results. Some of these may have been a little slow in showing themselves, but the pace of life is definitely increasing and you will need to keep your wits about you if you want to make the most of everything that is on offer. Don't forget about the needs of family members and your partner.

31 SATURDAY ☿ *Moon Age Day 11 Moon Sign Gemini*

Social and leisure pursuits probably demand more from you than you realise. This is especially true as far as your purse or wallet is concerned. If you take a little time you can think up things to do that hardly cost you anything at all. What is more, these turn out to be more enjoyable than any expensive adventure.

February

2015

1 SUNDAY ☿ *Moon Age Day 12 Moon Sign Cancer*

It is clearly your intention to be noticed today, but it would be sensible not to overdo it. You have a great element of fun about your nature and will also be good when it comes to intimate situations. What you don't have in abundance – for today at least – is quite the level of common sense that would be appropriate.

2 MONDAY ☿ *Moon Age Day 13 Moon Sign Cancer*

There ought to be many pleasant things happening as far as your romantic life is concerned. Established relationships strengthen under present trends and for Aquarians who are looking for new love, this is the time to focus your attention. Some of the affection that comes your way could be surprising.

3 TUESDAY ☿ *Moon Age Day 14 Moon Sign Leo*

Leave any grandiose schemes alone, at least for a couple of days until the lunar low has come and gone. Rest and relax, whilst at the same time bearing things in mind that you want to do later. In romantic clinches, you will find that normal reactions have to be modified.

4 WEDNESDAY ☿ *Moon Age Day 15 Moon Sign Leo*

Be as adaptable as possible today and don't expect to make much progress. As long as you recognise that the brakes are on and that there is little you can do about it for now, you will settle back and enjoy the break. Routines can now seem quite comforting, even ones that generally bore you.

5 THURSDAY ☿ *Moon Age Day 16 Moon Sign Leo*

Today brings a great deal of mental activity where your job is concerned. Most of your efforts at the moment are given over to the practical aspects of life and you won't be at all put out by working on several different fronts at the same time. The only slight fly in the ointment is that you are not as committed to relationships as you could be.

6 FRIDAY ☿ *Moon Age Day 17 Moon Sign Virgo*

Along comes a real intellectual peak during which you are able to express your originality and to make a tremendous impression on the world as a result. People like your slightly unusual look and the fact that you wear what you like. Aquarius doesn't follow fashion at the moment, it makes it.

7 SATURDAY ☿ *Moon Age Day 18 Moon Sign Virgo*

You need to be attentive and understanding in the domestic sphere. It could be that your nearest and dearest have got it into their heads that you either don't care or aren't interested in something. This has probably come about because you have been so busy in other directions. Now is the time to prove your concern.

8 SUNDAY ☿ *Moon Age Day 19 Moon Sign Libra*

You are quite charming at present and will be generally looking and feeling at your best. You have a number of very positive planetary positions and aspects at the moment and could easily be turning your mind towards romance on this very promising and eventful Sunday.

9 MONDAY ☿ *Moon Age Day 20 Moon Sign Libra*

It could seem more important to you today to look ahead at what you want to do, whilst ignoring what is truly important in an overall sense now. Try to concentrate on the matter at hand and don't be distracted by things that seem to sparkle on the horizon. Enlist the support of friends for specific purposes.

10 TUESDAY ☿ *Moon Age Day 21 Moon Sign Libra*

You now have more personal power to influence events, even if you don't necessarily realise the fact early in the day. Move forward cautiously, but there is nothing wrong with taking the odd calculated risk. This is a strange sort of day, because everything is working for you except your confidence.

11 WEDNESDAY ☿ *Moon Age Day 22 Moon Sign Scorpio*

Friends are supportive and stimulating on a day that is like to work extremely well for Aquarius. You show great diplomacy when it matters the most and can easily modify your own nature to accommodate the peculiarities of others. Most people will simply love to have you around.

12 THURSDAY ☿ *Moon Age Day 23 Moon Sign Scorpio*

People in your domestic sphere seem to be keeping you on your toes right now and you will have to give them at least some of your attention. Younger people especially make demands of you and will tax even your ability to show genuine empathy. On the other hand, if you think folk are wrong maybe you should tell them.

13 FRIDAY ☿ *Moon Age Day 24 Moon Sign Sagittarius*

During this period you seem to have marvellous ideas for achieving more financial strength, which in turn leads to a greater sense of independence. There is nothing wrong with experimenting with innovative ways of increasing your wealth, but stay away from get-rich-quick schemes that you sense are not worthwhile.

14 SATURDAY *Moon Age Day 25 Moon Sign Sagittarius*

There is likely to be a peak in your fortunes, particularly in a career sense. This might not be too obvious on a Saturday, but there are other benefits about, too. You are very motivated at present and quite keen to try something new. This will be especially the case if the weather seems to be improving and you can get out.

15 SUNDAY   *Moon Age Day 26 Moon Sign Capricorn*

The emphasis shifts now to having fun and you will be less concerned with the practical aspects of life that have been so significant earlier this month. Self-expression is important, as is the creative side of your nature. This should be a very interesting period and one that sees you making progress on several fronts.

16 MONDAY   *Moon Age Day 27 Moon Sign Capricorn*

You may well start the week filled with a desire for new experiences. There is plenty to be done and you remain very practical in your approach to life. Dealing with quieter people could prove to be something of a problem, but you have what it takes to bring almost anyone out of their shell.

17 TUESDAY   *Moon Age Day 28 Moon Sign Aquarius*

The green light is now on and you need to make as much headway as you can whilst the lunar high is around. When the Moon enters your zodiac sign it's time for business and you act positively through most areas of your life. Don't be surprised if people automatically turn to you for advice.

18 WEDNESDAY   *Moon Age Day 29 Moon Sign Aquarius*

What seems most important right now is your ability to focus on specific goals. It would be all too easy to dissipate the energy you have, but it would be far more useful to pick one or two tasks and tackle them to the best of your ability. Lady Luck should lend a definite hand today.

19 THURSDAY   *Moon Age Day 0 Moon Sign Pisces*

You can turn professional matters to your advantage at the moment and will be quite happy to look at new possibilities that could mean a change in responsibilities. Try to stay cool, calm and collected, even on those occasions when there is some provocation about. Routines are necessary, if somewhat tedious.

20 FRIDAY
Moon Age Day 1 Moon Sign Pisces

This is a time of strong intellectual insights and a period during which you are more likely to respond to gut reactions rather than simply to common sense. Pay attention when a little bell rings at the back of your mind. There could be some slight financial gains around and today should be generally rewarding.

21 SATURDAY
Moon Age Day 2 Moon Sign Aries

Major initiatives and moneymaking schemes are around, but whether or not you decide to become involved in them today depends mainly on your overall attitude. The social trends are strong and you may make up your mind that it would be better to dump some of the practical needs of the day in favour of having fun.

22 SUNDAY
Moon Age Day 3 Moon Sign Aries

The best thing you can do today is to get busy. Everything points to an active and enterprising time and you have what it takes to turn heads. Don't be in the least bit surprised today to discover that you have an admirer – and don't even be astonished if you find out that there is more than one!

23 MONDAY
Moon Age Day 4 Moon Sign Aries

Make family matters lively and rewarding, but leave issues related to domestic finances alone for the next couple of days. You should show your nearest and dearest that you know how to have fun and that you are considerate of their needs, too. Relatives can be friends, as well and you need to show that this is the case.

24 TUESDAY
Moon Age Day 5 Moon Sign Taurus

You should have great self-assurance today and a desire to get things right first time. Beware, though, that not everyone is going to be in the same frame of mind and if you have any difficulty at all it might be in persuading others to follow your lead. Friends prove to be very important and practical matters are not your only considerations today.

25 WEDNESDAY   *Moon Age Day 6 Moon Sign Taurus*

Don't take too much for granted today. You would be well advised to check and double-check all details, especially when it comes to travel of any sort. You would enjoy getting away from things and will be much inspired intellectually by almost any change of scene.

26 THURSDAY   *Moon Age Day 7 Moon Sign Gemini*

You now have great power to change things, even if you do so in small increments. Although you are neither pushy nor argumentative, you can still get your own way most of the time. Beware of small mishaps later in the day, because the Moon is not too far away from your opposite sign of Leo.

27 FRIDAY   *Moon Age Day 8 Moon Sign Gemini*

Beneficial trends at home remain your major focus for the moment. This could be a good time to get started on any changes or improvements you have in mind. What won't impress you right now will be other people's rules and regulations and you will react strongly if pushed.

28 SATURDAY   *Moon Age Day 9 Moon Sign Cancer*

You are in the midst of a rather busy phase at work, and this tends to apply whether you work at the weekend or not. When you are not actually involved in your career you will probably be thinking about it, but you should also take some time to yourself and explore social possibilities with friends.

March

2015

1 SUNDAY
Moon Age Day 10 Moon Sign Cancer

Bringing others round to your point of view won't be hard, because you have such winning ways. Another gift is your ability to weigh up the nature of the people with whom you are dealing in an instant. Addressing those around you in exactly the right way gains you significant dividends now.

2 MONDAY
Moon Age Day 11 Moon Sign Leo

This is an inauspicious time where finances are concerned, so your interests are best served by focusing on matters that have little or nothing to do with money. A good deal of thought goes into your plans for the future and this is the sphere of life that proves to be most rewarding whilst the lunar low is around.

3 TUESDAY
Moon Age Day 12 Moon Sign Leo

Things are still not quite as you would wish, but it won't be long now before you are back to normal. Someone you don't see too often could be making a return visit to your life and could bring surprises and a tendency to be somewhat nostalgic. By later tomorrow, you will be back on top form.

4 WEDNESDAY
Moon Age Day 13 Moon Sign Leo

The vigorous pursuit of romance and pleasure is what drives you at the moment. You are fun-loving and as generous as the day is long, which certainly gains you new friends. You typify the best of Aquarius in just about every way right now, and without the level of indecisiveness that you might have displayed recently.

86

5 THURSDAY
Moon Age Day 14 Moon Sign Virgo

Any sort of social activity is well starred now and you should be able to get more of what you want from life generally. There is nothing wrong with mixing business with pleasure, but remember to consider the feelings of those with whom you come into contact.

6 FRIDAY
Moon Age Day 15 Moon Sign Virgo

Today there is a great deal of personal energy about and your ego makes you inclined to shoot from the hip in almost any sort of company. There's nothing wrong with this, just as long as you have what it takes to back up your statements. Routines will seem a terrible bore and you may try to avoid them.

7 SATURDAY
Moon Age Day 16 Moon Sign Libra

This is the best time during March to try out new ideas and to show the world what you are capable of. If those around you were in any doubt about your abilities they probably will not be by the end of today. You are filled with character at this time and enjoy significant popularity with just about everyone.

8 SUNDAY
Moon Age Day 17 Moon Sign Libra

You need to keep your eyes and ears open as far as your personal ambitions are concerned. There is everything to play for and good luck may come into play. Routines are not for you at present. You will want to expand your horizons as much as possible and to try out new things.

9 MONDAY
Moon Age Day 18 Moon Sign Libra

Today you can make the greatest gains from the people who are naturally close to you. Whilst this clearly includes your partner and family members, you might be most reliant on a friend and will be leaning heavily upon them in some way. Standard responses probably won't work in social settings.

10 TUESDAY
Moon Age Day 19 Moon Sign Scorpio

Try to avoid getting overburdened with pointless tasks today. Social and personal possibilities are highlighted, but you won't recognise them if you spend all your time sorting things out. You remain active and enterprising, even if some of the people around you definitely are not.

11 WEDNESDAY
Moon Age Day 20 Moon Sign Scorpio

You have great potential for achievement at work and a knowing knack for being in the right place at the best possible time today. You show a greater effort where long-term goals are concerned and should also be enjoying the improving weather. Look out for the first signs of spring all around you.

12 THURSDAY
Moon Age Day 21 Moon Sign Sagittarius

This would be a very good day to spend at least a few hours with your partner or close personal friends. It is likely that you will become bored if you give yourself exclusively to work or practical matters. Others are definitely looking out for you now and show their concern at every turn.

13 FRIDAY
Moon Age Day 22 Moon Sign Sagittarius

Intellectual activities are now favourably highlighted. You show an interest in acquiring knowledge more or less for its own sake and you soak up facts and figures quite easily. This is likely to be a very busy day, but one during which you manage to achieve something that has been eluding you.

14 SATURDAY
Moon Age Day 23 Moon Sign Sagittarius

Joint finances look good right now and the weekend could give you the chance to discuss such matters with your partner or family members. There may be a stranger in your social midst around now, but with a little effort on your part this is a person who could soon become a firm and treasured friend.

15 SUNDAY
Moon Age Day 24 Moon Sign Capricorn

You are much admired at the moment and will be lapping up the compliments at every turn. The only slight problem is that you could get too big for your own boots, a difficulty that doesn't come along often for Aquarian people. Friends should be able to show you an entirely different side of life now.

16 MONDAY
Moon Age Day 25 Moon Sign Capricorn

You will work very hard this week, and not because other people expect you to do so. Aquarius is entering a very determined stage and you won't take kindly to anyone ordering you about. Carry on living your life the way that suits you, rather than wasting time reacting.

17 TUESDAY
Moon Age Day 26 Moon Sign Aquarius

You should easily be able to spot opportunities almost instantly today and the lunar high is likely to pep things up no end. With everything to play for in the financial and career stakes, you get what you want most of the time and will be looking ahead well, too. Strike whilst the iron is hot where romance is concerned.

18 WEDNESDAY
Moon Age Day 27 Moon Sign Aquarius

Today's influences indicate that you are able to call the shots and you won't ease the pressure until you go to bed again. It might seem as if this could be something of a trial, but you clearly respond well and soak up the pressure like a sponge at the moment.

19 THURSDAY
Moon Age Day 28 Moon Sign Pisces

You can expect a brisk general pace to life, which is, after all, the way you like things to be. You push forward mainly under your own steam and aren't restrained by the actions or opinions of others. There may be moments you need help, but there is just a danger you will be too proud to ask for it.

20 FRIDAY
Moon Age Day 0 Moon Sign Pisces

You could be in a better position to attract money than has been the case for a number of weeks. It isn't so much what you do right now that matters, but more the effort you have put in previously. Be careful, though, because cash can run through your hands like water.

21 SATURDAY
Moon Age Day 1 Moon Sign Aries

Your mind is very sharp and ideas are flowing well for you at the moment. Active and enterprising, you also have what it takes to make money. At the same time, you have to remember that this is a Saturday. You owe some time to the people you don't see as much as you might during the week.

22 SUNDAY
Moon Age Day 2 Moon Sign Aries

You attract people right now and will be mixing with individuals who have what it takes to move your life forward in some way. There are some gains to be made in the practical sphere of life, but as this is a Sunday you will probably want to spend some time with family members, especially with your romantic partner.

23 MONDAY
Moon Age Day 3 Moon Sign Taurus

You are spending a good deal of your time working hard, but you also show a desire to change things to your advantage at home. It will have occurred to you that the year is growing older and the days are getting longer. The arrival of spring could be sufficient incentive to make alterations at home.

24 TUESDAY
Moon Age Day 4 Moon Sign Taurus

Family trends look very good and there are small rewards coming in. These could be of a financial nature as a result of moves you made in the past. There is no harm in feeling a little nostalgic on the odd occasion, but you would do well to remind yourself that there is no future in the past.

25 WEDNESDAY   *Moon Age Day 5 Moon Sign Gemini*

Variety and warmth in equal quantities could make this day rather special. Don't get too involved with matters that have nothing to do with you and curb that curiosity if you don't want to get bogged down in someone else's mire. There is enough to do today keeping yourself tuned in to what lies ahead.

26 THURSDAY   *Moon Age Day 6 Moon Sign Gemini*

Your thoughts are now set on widening your horizons as much as you can. Some of this has to do with work, but there may also be a strong desire for travel. It might prove difficult to go very far for now, but you can plan ahead. For now, even short excursions would do you a great deal of good.

27 FRIDAY   *Moon Age Day 7 Moon Sign Cancer*

Financial and practical matters receive a good deal of input, but you may not be in the right frame of mind to deal with it. Shelve things you don't want to sort out today and enjoy some time spent either alone or with one very special person. Trying to bulldoze situations at the moment simply will not work.

28 SATURDAY   *Moon Age Day 8 Moon Sign Cancer*

You will be very expressive and outgoing today. All traces of the hesitation and doubt that were evident a few days ago should have disappeared and you know exactly how to get what you want in most situations. Aquarius is very attractive at the moment and that means you are in the limelight.

29 SUNDAY   *Moon Age Day 9 Moon Sign Cancer*

It looks as though there is a strong desire for personal freedom and you can be quite fidgety if you don't have the chance to follow your own desires today. Travel and cultural matters are of great significance, and the strong intellectual qualities you possess make you shy away from anything that seems ignorant or lacking in finesse.

30 MONDAY *Moon Age Day 10 Moon Sign Leo*

Current trends suggest that you can make the best of offers that come in from outside. These may have a bearing on your work and it is likely that you show yourself to be more than capable now in whatever you choose to take on. Romance is also on the cards for young or young-at-heart Aquarians.

31 TUESDAY *Moon Age Day 11 Moon Sign Leo*

Your capacity for clear-sightedness now sets you apart in the estimation of others, which is why you might feel like an agony aunt before the end of the day. It is unlikely that you will complain much, because it is good to know that people trust you and that they think you have the answers they need.

April

2015

1 WEDNESDAY
Moon Age Day 12 Moon Sign Virgo

There is potential today to further your financial aims. You are able to look ahead with confidence and can manipulate situations and bring them round to your own way of thinking. Getting family members to do your bidding is likely to be somewhat more complicated.

2 THURSDAY
Moon Age Day 13 Moon Sign Virgo

Everything that is really important and meaningful about today centres on personal relationships and the way you are viewing them. Do everything you can to make your partner happy; and if you don't have a partner at the moment, you could just be in the best position to find one.

3 FRIDAY
Moon Age Day 14 Moon Sign Virgo

A boost to all communication issues is now at hand and you won't have any difficulty getting your message across, even when it's a complicated one. How good you would be in debates or in any situation where you are put on the spot! The only slight problem is that you don't have as much regard for yourself as others do for you.

4 SATURDAY
Moon Age Day 15 Moon Sign Libra

The chances are you will be happy with the general pace of life and still gaining a great deal, thanks to the attitude and actions of loved ones. This might not be the best financial day of the month, but you tend to hold on to what you have and can lay down plans for future monetary improvements.

5 SUNDAY
Moon Age Day 16 Moon Sign Libra

This would be a very good time to focus your attention on creative pursuits. People are anxious to be on your side and you could find that you are being put in charge of certain situations. Trying to balance the needs of those you really care about might prove a little difficult, but you should manage well enough.

6 MONDAY
Moon Age Day 17 Moon Sign Scorpio

You seem quite restless now and might find it difficult to settle to routines. Aquarius has a need to break out and to look at life in quite a different way. Meetings with new and inspiring people are on the cards and you are also quite sensitive to the needs of family members, especially those who are younger than you.

7 TUESDAY
Moon Age Day 18 Moon Sign Scorpio

You need to be especially careful today with jobs that need a very delicate touch. Aquarius is now inclined to go at things like a bull at a gate and that could lead to some significant problems. With everything now on offer in a social sense, it is clear that play is more important than work at present.

8 WEDNESDAY
Moon Age Day 19 Moon Sign Scorpio

You remain generally optimistic, which is the best way for Aquarius to be. Getting other people to follow suit won't be at all easy and it is plain that there are some real old grumps around at the moment. Try to ignore them and carry on in your own sweet way.

9 THURSDAY
Moon Age Day 20 Moon Sign Sagittarius

Projects that started some time ago are likely to come to fruition under present trends, but you could find slight delays in more practical matters, probably because it is hard to get anyone else motivated right now. Asking for what you want seems to be the best way forward, even if you tend to embarrass yourself on the way.

10 FRIDAY   *Moon Age Day 21   Moon Sign Sagittarius*

Perhaps you need to rid yourself of some dead wood and to be thinking about newer and better ways of tackling old situations. Money matters should ease and there could even be a few pounds around that you didn't expect to have. Casual conversations can lead to quite significant realisations on your part.

11 SATURDAY   *Moon Age Day 22   Moon Sign Capricorn*

Look out for a few financial drawbacks. You might have to be more careful about what you are spending, but keep your eyes open for a bargain. People who have not figured in your life for quite some time could be putting in a renewed appearance at any time now.

12 SUNDAY   *Moon Age Day 23   Moon Sign Capricorn*

Strive to reduce any responsibilities that seem particularly heavy by persuading others to take some of the strain. Since most of what you are worrying about is not your personal business in any case, it's only fair that those around you should take some of the burden. Things will change quickly.

13 MONDAY   *Moon Age Day 24   Moon Sign Aquarius*

The new working week opens with a real flourish and the lunar high offers you all manner of new incentives that seem to come along at just the right time. Although you may be fighting off one or two problems from the past, you are now in the best position possible to sort these out.

14 TUESDAY   *Moon Age Day 25   Moon Sign Aquarius*

You now have all the energy you could need in order to accomplish personal goals. There is plenty of help around if you need it, but it is most likely that you choose to rely almost entirely on yourself. This is not to imply that you ignore those around you, because you are really very sociable.

15 WEDNESDAY
Moon Age Day 26 Moon Sign Pisces

Don't avoid taking major decisions today just because you are worried that you could upset someone else. It would be difficult to achieve anything without treading on a few toes, but as long as you explain yourself first you have the right to make up your own mind. Keep talking to colleagues and your boss.

16 THURSDAY
Moon Age Day 27 Moon Sign Pisces

There are signs that you could be entering a week of fits and starts where your career is concerned. If you really want to get on, it will be important to deal with matters one at a time and to make sure each is sorted before you move on. Things are less problematical in personal attachments, which look entirely secure now.

17 FRIDAY
Moon Age Day 28 Moon Sign Aries

You remain generally optimistic and able to get others to do your bidding without bullying them in any way. You often show a great interest for the old, curious or downright odd, and this definitely seems to be the case at the moment. Keep a watchful eye on spending and curb the extravagant tendencies of others.

18 SATURDAY
Moon Age Day 29 Moon Sign Aries

The weekend should be steady, though the pace can be stepped up if you fancy a more eventful time. It is most likely that you will be content to watch and wait, or to go shopping. Aquarius loves luxury and this certainly seems to be the case at the moment. You show yourself to be very sensitive in personal attachments.

19 SUNDAY
Moon Age Day 0 Moon Sign Taurus

This is likely to be the start of a very good period on the home front and a time when your mind naturally turns in the direction of ways to make yourself more comfortable. There are some slight financial gains in the offing, even if these come not as a result of your own efforts but as a result of luck.

20 MONDAY
Moon Age Day 1 Moon Sign Taurus

Your ability to communicate your true feelings to loved ones is very well marked today. If you know very well that a heart-to-heart is long overdue, you could do worse than to instigate it some time today. You have a light touch when dealing with subordinates or younger family members.

21 TUESDAY
Moon Age Day 2 Moon Sign Gemini

Balancing your time commitments could prove to be rather difficult at this stage of the working week. It will seem as though everyone is demanding your attention during every minute. This would be a problem to some zodiac signs, but you have the mind of a juggler and can cope, even when the pressure is really on.

22 WEDNESDAY
Moon Age Day 3 Moon Sign Gemini

You really need to make room in your life for doing what you want, rather than what seems expedient. There are some interesting encounters on the way, some of which are likely to be totally unexpected. Don't be too quick to react to what sounds like an insult, because you could have things entirely wrong.

23 THURSDAY
Moon Age Day 4 Moon Sign Gemini

There could be some hold-ups today, so it would be advisable to deal with situations one at a time and make sure that you have achieved all you can before moving on. The attitude of colleagues and friends can be difficult to interpret and you might have to ask more questions than would usually be the case.

24 FRIDAY
Moon Age Day 5 Moon Sign Cancer

There is a continued positive focus on your family life, together with a real insight into the motivations of others generally. Your intuition is working well at the moment, so you might easily be able to guess how almost anyone will react. This can be a very fortunate gift when it comes to business.

25 SATURDAY
Moon Age Day 6 Moon Sign Cancer

Although you think quickly and react positively this weekend, there is also a dreamy side to your nature that seems to have little to do with your normal state of mind at the moment. You could also be very nostalgic and much more likely to hold on to precious memories than has been the case recently.

26 SUNDAY
Moon Age Day 7 Moon Sign Leo

It appears that you are just not up to certain tasks and you can blame the lunar low for this state of affairs. There are so many positive planetary positions surrounding you that it is uncertain how much you will notice this rather negative interlude, but you could find it difficult to concentrate on the matter at hand.

27 MONDAY
Moon Age Day 8 Moon Sign Leo

This is an inauspicious time to be taking risks, especially where cash is concerned. Instead, you should stick to what you know and keep life as moderate as possible. Friends may be more reactive and inclined to fly off the handle for no real reason.

28 TUESDAY
Moon Age Day 9 Moon Sign Leo

For the third day in a row the Moon is in your opposite zodiac sign, but not for too long. Things may start out quiet, but as the day progresses you will notice that you are feeling more like your old self. By the evening, you should be advertising your presence again and would be willing to be fully involved in social ventures.

29 WEDNESDAY
Moon Age Day 10 Moon Sign Virgo

With so much planetary energy focused on the positive things of life, no wonder you make a good impression in the middle of this week. Although you show great flexibility, it would still be sensible to stick in the main to what you know and understand. Much time can be lost simply coming to terms with new situations.

30 THURSDAY
Moon Age Day 11 Moon Sign Virgo

This is a good time for professional developments, and Aquarians who are between jobs need to keep their eyes wide open now. With everything to play for financially, you can find ways of increasing your income, even if the outcome of your present plans lies some way in the future.

May

2015

1 FRIDAY
Moon Age Day 12 Moon Sign Libra

It's the wonderful first of May and getting around socially is just what the doctor ordered for you at this time. You should certainly be feeling the pull of the season and will want to be involved in all activities you can. There is a good chance you will succeed at something that has been a problem in the past.

2 SATURDAY
Moon Age Day 13 Moon Sign Libra

This is a time for revitalising elements of your personal life. An emotional issue could be preoccupying you somewhat and there might even be the possibility of an argument that springs from a romantic attachment. Keep in touch with people who either live at a distance or those you simply don't see very often.

3 SUNDAY
Moon Age Day 14 Moon Sign Libra

On the whole, life ought to appear fairly stable today and there are likely to be very few contentious people around. With a peaceful period comes your desire to forge ahead and to get what you want in a material sense. The right words of love spoken this evening can have a marked bearing on the immediate future.

4 MONDAY
Moon Age Day 15 Moon Sign Scorpio

The pace of everyday life increases, so much so that you might have to run in order to keep up. Acting on impulse, you can probably get further at the moment than you usually can when you act cautiously. At least part of today should be spent with family members or friends who are especially dear to you.

5 TUESDAY
Moon Age Day 16 Moon Sign Scorpio

Someone may challenge you in a professional sense, but you have a broad back at the moment and can deal with this sort of situation easily enough. Not everything goes your way right now, but when it matters the most you have all the energy and determination needed to get you to the winning post.

6 WEDNESDAY
Moon Age Day 17 Moon Sign Sagittarius

You tend to be more in touch with others now and can easily understand how their minds are working. This sort of deep intuition is typical of your zodiac sign and it can be somewhat uncomfortable on occasions, because your empathy is so complete. Remember that you have your own life to live, too.

7 THURSDAY
Moon Age Day 18 Moon Sign Sagittarius

This is a wonderful time to be with others and to enjoy the positive trends that are presently surrounding you. You can be more or less certain to give a good impression and your popularity is likely to be high. If there is something you want but you have been afraid to ask for it, this would be the best time to have a go.

8 FRIDAY
Moon Age Day 19 Moon Sign Capricorn

Professional challenges could end the working week, but you will take these in your stride as surely as anything else that seems to take effort. With a real sense of urgency, you can now break down any red tape that impedes you and get to the heart of matters when you need to. Friends will be helpful.

9 SATURDAY
Moon Age Day 20 Moon Sign Capricorn

Your powers are somewhat limited at this time, but you should not allow this to get in the way too much. For today a twelfth house Moon keeps you pressed down and it will take an extra burst of effort on your part to get where you really want to be. Stick to enjoying yourself and avoid professional matters.

10 SUNDAY
Moon Age Day 21 Moon Sign Aquarius

Your personal strengths put in a very definite appearance today and you should discover capabilities you didn't even know you had. Use the lunar high to get ahead in any way you can, but specifically concentrate on the possibility of advancement at work. You will simply want to have fun this evening.

11 MONDAY
Moon Age Day 22 Moon Sign Aquarius

This is the time of the month that focuses on you getting what you want from life. Your powers of persuasion are good and it should not be at all difficult to bring others round to your point of view. Although family members might be arguing, you play the honest broker and can do some important problem solving.

12 TUESDAY
Moon Age Day 23 Moon Sign Aquarius

Now you can enjoy a special time with someone you love a great deal. This is one of the best days of the month for romance and offers you the chance to find exactly the right words. A slightly embarrassing situation could occur if someone you never suspected tells you how important you are to them.

13 WEDNESDAY
Moon Age Day 24 Moon Sign Pisces

You encounter the new and the unusual in almost anything you undertake at the moment and will be quite pleased to stretch credibility on a number of different occasions. Avoid arguing for your limitations, but believe yourself to be capable of anything. You won't be, but it's a start.

14 THURSDAY
Moon Age Day 25 Moon Sign Pisces

This would be an excellent time to further your education in some way and it is likely that many Aquarians will be thinking in terms of improving themselves. Don't be too critical of the behaviour of a family member. You can't see into another's soul and perhaps don't know all the details surrounding his or her life.

15 FRIDAY
Moon Age Day 26 Moon Sign Aries

Beware of being too rash for your own good. The problem is that you are likely to speak out without thinking much in advance. This could land you in some hot water and you will need to react quickly in order to get out of trouble. Fortunately, you are well equipped for thinking on your feet.

16 SATURDAY
Moon Age Day 27 Moon Sign Aries

This might be the best day of the month to ask something of a friend or a family member. Not only do you have a good deal of cheek, but you are also blessed with strong persuasive powers. Doing favours for others comes quite naturally and you will also be very tidy-minded at present.

17 SUNDAY
Moon Age Day 28 Moon Sign Taurus

A domestic relationship or some situation within your immediate vicinity is likely to become more of an issue today. You will require flexibility and understanding in order to deal well with others and need to exhibit more patience. Any nagging doubts you feel today probably have no basis in fact.

18 MONDAY
Moon Age Day 0 Moon Sign Taurus

You are entering a week that has a great deal to offer in a social sense and although you will be applying yourself very well at work, it is those hours you spend away from responsibility that are likely to be the most rewarding. Energy levels remain variable, especially beyond the middle of the week.

19 TUESDAY
☿ *Moon Age Day 1 Moon Sign Gemini*

When you are faced with something that genuinely interests you, it should be easy to race for the finishing line. The same cannot be said of jobs that you see as boring or without purpose. Whenever you can, you are likely to leave such things to others. Beware of leaving yourself open to accusations of laziness.

20 WEDNESDAY ☿   *Moon Age Day 2 Moon Sign Gemini*

It might seem as though certain circumstances are working against your best interests now, but this isn't necessarily the case. Look at things from a different angle and try to be both original and inventive. It won't be long before you discover that you can turn misfortune in your direction.

21 THURSDAY ☿   *Moon Age Day 3 Moon Sign Cancer*

Compromise is very important at this stage of the week. The position of the planet Mars in your solar chart can make you somewhat obstinate and less inclined to seek a path that is both reasonable and realistic. Despite the difficulties, you need to avoid going out on a limb or committing yourself to too many jobs.

22 FRIDAY ☿   *Moon Age Day 4 Moon Sign Cancer*

Although positive and new possibilities are in evidence all around you, for the moment you don't feel inclined to become involved. Treat the coming few days as being nothing more than an interlude during which you have time to contemplate life. Everyone needs a break now and again and Aquarius is no exception.

23 SATURDAY ☿   *Moon Age Day 5 Moon Sign Leo*

Extra work seems to be the order of today, but what is really happening is that the arrival of the lunar low is making you look at things rather negatively. Allow others to take some of the strain and don't be too quick off the mark with new plans. It might be better to leave significant plans until after the weekend.

24 SUNDAY ☿   *Moon Age Day 6 Moon Sign Leo*

You could be rather suspicious of the motives of other people and that can make for a rather uncomfortable day in some respects. It would be best to give almost everyone the benefit of the doubt, though without surrendering control altogether. Better trends are on the way.

25 MONDAY ☿ *Moon Age Day 7 Moon Sign Leo*

Practical issues should be easier to deal with now and you show a great deal of tolerance when dealing with others. Colleagues are likely to be quite demanding, but you look to their humanity and will be showing great sensitivity to the needs of others generally. Routines can be a drag, but they may be necessary.

26 TUESDAY ☿ *Moon Age Day 8 Moon Sign Virgo*

New ideas and changed perspectives are nothing new to the average Aquarian. Today, you excel when it comes to looking at alternatives and you carry the opinions of others with you because of your powers of persuasion. Keep in touch with people who may be far away from you at present.

27 WEDNESDAY ☿ *Moon Age Day 9 Moon Sign Virgo*

Though optimism might seem to be in abundance, you are somewhat hesitant at the moment. You need constant reassurance from others and will be checking the attitude of family members and friends on a very regular basis. Get organised where family obligations are concerned.

28 THURSDAY ☿ *Moon Age Day 10 Moon Sign Libra*

There is a chance that you will have to deal with some restlessness that is rising within your nature at present. Staying put and concentrating on the same old things won't appeal to you at all. It could be the arrival of the early summer or simply symptomatic of the period, but whatever the cause you feel the need to move.

29 FRIDAY ☿ *Moon Age Day 11 Moon Sign Libra*

Be bold brave and determined when faced with some sort of challenge. This won't be difficult because you are clearly in the market for stretching yourself – though, once again, only when it suits your purposes to do so. You certainly will not take kindly to being told what to do by anyone today.

30 SATURDAY ☿ *Moon Age Day 12 Moon Sign Libra*

Success comes more easily to you today and you will be right on form, especially when in company. You relish the presence of interesting and informative people in your life and will be working hard to achieve specific objectives. Most important of all you find it easier to concentrate now.

31 SUNDAY ☿ *Moon Age Day 13 Moon Sign Scorpio*

This is an excellent time to be out in the social mainstream, impressing people and making new friends. Don't get over-confident if you happen to be at work and be willing to settle for second-best in at least one case. All in all, you are better off tackling situations one at a time and head on whenever possible at present.

June

2015

1 MONDAY
☿ *Moon Age Day 14 Moon Sign Scorpio*

What you really epitomise at the moment is effectiveness. Whatever you decide to turn your hand to is likely to be accomplished quickly and without any undue fuss. You will need to be on the ball when it comes to dealing with wayward family members later in the day, but you also show significant patience now.

2 TUESDAY
☿ *Moon Age Day 15 Moon Sign Sagittarius*

You need to own up to your responsibility in a certain area of life, even though to do so might seem rather embarrassing. Getting your point of view across is not quite so easy now as it was a couple of days ago and it might seem that certain people are doing everything they can to get in your way.

3 WEDNESDAY
☿ *Moon Age Day 16 Moon Sign Sagittarius*

Benefits are on offer today through relationships and right now you should be feeling a safe and secure bond with loved ones. There will be time for romance in your life, even though you may feel that practical matters are not being attended to. Tomorrow is another day, so for the moment simply enjoy being cosseted.

4 THURSDAY
☿ *Moon Age Day 17 Moon Sign Sagittarius*

If you are having difficulties with a friend or a social contact at the moment, you will be more inclined to turn towards your partner or family members. The attitude of colleagues needs some thinking about, but openly arguing with them won't achieve anything.

5 FRIDAY ☿ *Moon Age Day 18 Moon Sign Capricorn*

There are social bonuses to be had at present. Others will discover just how charming you can be and the best qualities of Aquarius are now shining through. You are likely to be looking for entertainment and will gain as a result of your ability to lead the field when it comes to having a good time.

6 SATURDAY ☿ *Moon Age Day 19 Moon Sign Capricorn*

This can be a time of intuitive awareness and a period during which you can easily assess the way others are likely to be thinking and acting. Although there are some delays to be dealt with at the moment, when it comes to getting others to do your bidding you have rarely been more successful.

7 SUNDAY ☿ *Moon Age Day 20 Moon Sign Aquarius*

There are signs that this could turn out to be the luckiest period of the month. The lunar high offers you the possibility of taking a few chances and you should discover that your decisions tend to be quick and useful. Don't stick with routines at the moment. Instead, try to alter your schedules as much as possible.

8 MONDAY ☿ *Moon Age Day 21 Moon Sign Aquarius*

You can have a tremendous influence over others at the moment and find it easy to bring them round to your point of view. It looks as though good fortune is on your side, which is why you are willing to take a few risks. Juggling work and pleasure ought not to be a problem today.

9 TUESDAY ☿ *Moon Age Day 22 Moon Sign Pisces*

This is a time during which you can reach out socially, probably in directions you hadn't really considered before. The attitude of some relatives is rather puzzling and you will certainly have more success with friends than family members. What could really irritate you at the moment are arrogant people, whom you tend to ignore.

10 WEDNESDAY ☿   *Moon Age Day 23 Moon Sign Pisces*

There is a warning today not to be too impulsive, which means you must avoid taking decisions that will have a bearing on your life for weeks or months to come. Don't sign documents now unless you have no choice. If there's really no choice, make sure you scrutinise the small print.

11 THURSDAY ☿   *Moon Age Day 24 Moon Sign Aries*

This could well be a very good time to plan a day away or even to take one at a moment's notice. You won't be all that happy to be kept in the same place all the time and can easily become bored with routines. There are potential gains to be made through casual contacts and unusual business deals.

12 FRIDAY ☿   *Moon Age Day 25 Moon Sign Aries*

Career matters are on a roll at the end of this working week and you can gain a great deal by simply being in the right place at the most opportune time. In a professional sense, you may be comparing notes with colleagues and will be in the right frame of mind to co-operate right across the board.

13 SATURDAY   *Moon Age Day 26 Moon Sign Taurus*

There could be encounters with potential new friends now and you should not turn down the chance to get together with likeminded people. The gregarious side of your nature is now clearly on display and you have what it takes to impress those who can do you some good in a financial sense.

14 SUNDAY   *Moon Age Day 27 Moon Sign Taurus*

Try to seek out new social contacts today. There are signs that this could be an important time to make new friends and you need to watch out in particular for people who are on the same mental wavelength as you. There could be a stop-start feeling to today that can only be countered by applying yourself fully to the task at hand.

15 MONDAY
Moon Age Day 28 Moon Sign Gemini

Today should put you in the picture regarding a specific objective and probably one that is of a personal nature. Your imagination might not be quite what you need it to be and as a result you will have some boring moments to go through. If time hangs heavy on your hands, seek out a friend in the evening.

16 TUESDAY
Moon Age Day 29 Moon Sign Gemini

Instead of firing from the hip when it comes to discussions or even arguments, listen carefully to what others are saying. Compromise is possible and you will do yourself a favour if you accept this fact. Aquarius can be very awkward to deal with today, but thankfully this is nothing but a short interlude.

17 WEDNESDAY
Moon Age Day 0 Moon Sign Cancer

You should now be on a roll and will want to do all you can to make the lot of your friends easier. You will also be on top form when it comes to romance. Compliments flow from you like honey and are likely to be well accepted, which is especially good if you are at the very beginning of a relationship.

18 THURSDAY
Moon Age Day 1 Moon Sign Cancer

You now tend to look towards those things that are both realistic and practical, and in this way you make headway with your life generally. Aquarius is not always this sensible, but it pays dividends when you are. Family members and friends alike should be clamouring for your attention at the moment.

19 FRIDAY
Moon Age Day 2 Moon Sign Cancer

Joint finances should be looking fairly good at the moment and you have it within you to organise yourself very well today. Life is likely to be fairly steady and your natural tendency to react positively to situations seems to be in place. Attitude is very important when dealing with professional matters.

20 SATURDAY
Moon Age Day 3 Moon Sign Leo

You can feel a little low whilst the Moon is in your opposite zodiac sign and will have to work fairly hard to overcome the everyday obstacles that life places in your path. Don't overreact to situations you know in your heart are only temporary. Instead, make plans for the second half of the week.

21 SUNDAY
Moon Age Day 4 Moon Sign Leo

Energy probably seems limited again today and it will appear that everyone else is getting ahead much more progressively than you are. This is not really the case at all; it's merely a matter of perspective. By tomorrow you are likely to be right back on form, so for the remainder of today find ways to amuse yourself.

22 MONDAY
Moon Age Day 5 Moon Sign Virgo

Though on a personal level you seem to be very boisterous, you also have it within you to be quiet and contemplative. This is a day that needs to be divided into compartments, and on which you can more easily come to terms with the attitudes and opinions of those with whom you live.

23 TUESDAY
Moon Age Day 6 Moon Sign Virgo

Today is good for communications and for getting to know people who might be of use to you a little further down the line. Be certain before you commit yourself to a major change; it might even be sensible to put such matters on hold for a day or two. You should be on top form, socially.

24 WEDNESDAY
Moon Age Day 7 Moon Sign Virgo

Now you can expect favourable trends associated with travel of any sort and you should also be very sharp when in company. Your active mind goes this way and that, and you respond very well to intellectual discussions and to anything associated with current affairs and your locality.

25 THURSDAY   *Moon Age Day 8 Moon Sign Libra*

Taking actions without sufficient consideration will lead you to slight problems for today at least. As is often the case, you need to be very careful and to address new situations as cautiously as you can. The start of new projects will have to wait until you are sure that they are what you need in order to progress.

26 FRIDAY   *Moon Age Day 9 Moon Sign Libra*

Certain information coming in from associates should prove to be very interesting today and you are likely to be back up to speed in no time at all. Even the most casual remark can set you thinking, and you seem to have what it takes to bring others round to your specific point of view without really trying.

27 SATURDAY   *Moon Age Day 10 Moon Sign Scorpio*

You seem to be on a definite winning streak, but you might have to back off in terms of career now that the weekend has arrived. Slowing your mind down won't be easy, which is why you need to keep it busy dealing with matters that are of personal rather than practical interest. Friends should be warm and receptive today.

28 SUNDAY   *Moon Age Day 11 Moon Sign Scorpio*

It seems that you can get a great deal from a range of different people at present and you are unlikely to be looking at anything too deeply. The reason for this lies in the fact that there is so much around that takes your interest. You tend to be a grazer at the moment, especially on new facts that surround your life.

29 MONDAY   *Moon Age Day 12 Moon Sign Scorpio*

Positive influences surround you on all sides, making the start of a new working week an ideal period in which to push yourself a little more. You don't know what you are capable of achieving until you try and there should be ample opportunity to flex your business muscles over the next few days.

30 TUESDAY   *Moon Age Day 13 Moon Sign Sagittarius*

Emotional attachments should now prove to be warmer and more secure than ever and you may not really want to move far from home today. Once you have made a move, you will settle to whatever you have to do very well. However, you might not show quite the flexibility of nature that often typifies the average Aquarian.

July
2015

1 WEDNESDAY   *Moon Age Day 14 Moon Sign Sagittarius*

Review past efforts for the best chance of getting ahead right now. Contributing to your own eventual success is possible, but you won't get everything you want without relying on others more than has been the case recently. Confidence is high in some matters, but distinctly lacking in others.

2 THURSDAY   *Moon Age Day 15 Moon Sign Capricorn*

Someone special has a message or two for you. This might be a slightly frustrating day in one way or another, not least because the people you rely on a professional sense are either missing or not performing to the best of their ability. Attitude is very important in practical matters.

3 FRIDAY   *Moon Age Day 16 Moon Sign Capricorn*

Personalities entering your life now could bring with them the chance for you to get something you have wanted for a while. Your attitude is very important today. You can get almost anything if you show the world at large that you know what you are doing and that you are trustworthy.

4 SATURDAY   *Moon Age Day 17 Moon Sign Aquarius*

The lunar high offers you the chance to get ahead of the pack and to make a good impression when it counts the most. However, you won't want to be spending all day doing practical things. There is fun to be had and you know just the right people to draw into your present schemes.

5 SUNDAY
Moon Age Day 18 Moon Sign Aquarius

Lady Luck is on your side again and a few calculated gambles could probably turn out much better than you would have expected. A little cheek goes a long way – and you have plenty at the moment. Your popularity is high and it won't be at all difficult to get what you want in almost any field of endeavour.

6 MONDAY
Moon Age Day 19 Moon Sign Pisces

It is possible for you to put your practical thoughts into words that the world understands. Not only this, but it also appears that certain of your colleagues and even superiors might be actively seeking you out. Stay away from situations over which you can have no influence and which might prove awkward.

7 TUESDAY
Moon Age Day 20 Moon Sign Pisces

This is an excellent day to be out and about, because there are signs that influences surrounding you are changing all the time. The home bird now disappears and you are at your very best when there are adventures about. In a social sense, you now have what it takes to paint the town red.

8 WEDNESDAY
Moon Age Day 21 Moon Sign Aries

You might be sought after now because of your leadership qualities and people are certainly likely to follow your lead. For this reason, you have to show great consideration for their welfare, too, and this might prove just a little tiresome. There ought to be some interesting social interludes later in the day.

9 THURSDAY
Moon Age Day 22 Moon Sign Aries

Those higher up the professional tree than you are might prove to be especially useful at the moment, but only because of your positive and helpful attitude. Personalities are apt to enter your life around now and bring with them some interesting potential changes of direction for you.

10 FRIDAY
Moon Age Day 23 Moon Sign Taurus

Challenges and career moves are easy to deal with and this is a time during which you don't mind at all taking on new responsibilities. You can be very impressive when in company, so don't be surprised if others are paying you some significant compliments. Present trends are also good when it comes to love and romance.

11 SATURDAY
Moon Age Day 24 Moon Sign Taurus

Most friendship issues are positively highlighted and it ought to be a piece of cake to get others to do your bidding. Not that you are being selfish, because most of your present intentions suit others as much as they do you. This will be a socially rewarding day for most, with plenty of romantic possibilities, too.

12 SUNDAY
Moon Age Day 25 Moon Sign Taurus

It could feel that your emotional security is being threatened in some way, but avoid hanging on to the past. If you project your mind forward, you can make slow and steady progress. Anything old is of particular interest to you at the moment and you can gain by visiting art galleries or museums.

13 MONDAY
Moon Age Day 26 Moon Sign Gemini

Professional circles bring new friendships and new ways of looking at old situations. What is most noticeable at the moment is the way you cut through red tape and get to the heart of any matter. People will be pleased to follow your lead at the moment, so the time has come to put a few plans into action.

14 TUESDAY
Moon Age Day 27 Moon Sign Gemini

This is still a good time for getting those around you to follow your lead and to do what you think is best. You don't need to waste time explaining yourself, because your actions speak louder than any words could. Personalities abound and there is no doubt that you are now chief amongst them.

15 WEDNESDAY *Moon Age Day 28 Moon Sign Cancer*

Although you are still enjoying the backing of others in matters associated with work, family members won't be half so accommodating. You show a great ability to help the world at large and your social conscience is well marked at the moment. Confidence is variable, but strong when you are supporting others.

16 THURSDAY *Moon Age Day 0 Moon Sign Cancer*

You should not be short of interesting company and for many this part of the working week brings with it some fascinating possibilities for later. Once work is out of the way, set out to enjoy yourself. The evening can prove to be extremely entertaining, partly because you are at your amusing best.

17 FRIDAY *Moon Age Day 1 Moon Sign Leo*

Progress is apt to be rather slow whilst the lunar low is around, so much so that today and tomorrow mark a time during which you ought to be thinking rather than doing. Don't be too quick to take on anything new and you certainly should not be pushing the bounds of the possible until the far end of the weekend.

18 SATURDAY *Moon Age Day 2 Moon Sign Leo*

Keep to tried and tested methods of doing things, because the new and radical is not the way forward at the moment. The greatest happiness today comes from being close to those you love, many of whom will be actively putting themselves out in order to make you happy. Routines might seem comfortable.

19 SUNDAY *Moon Age Day 3 Moon Sign Leo*

It might seem in some ways that home is the best place to be today, though you won't take much persuading otherwise. If that is the case, you will be gadding about again and may take special pleasure from shopping or visiting a place of historic or scenic interest.

20 MONDAY
Moon Age Day 4 Moon Sign Virgo

The emphasis at the moment seems to be on one-to-one relationships and you may be spending some time looking at how you can improve them. Family concerns are also likely to be uppermost in your mind and although you have what it takes to work hard, your mind may often be elsewhere.

21 TUESDAY
Moon Age Day 5 Moon Sign Virgo

Although most aspects of life should now seem fairly settled, your emotional responses might be somewhat odd. You don't get the messages from your partner that you might expect and could in any case be rather more sensitive than is good for you. Avoid taking things too seriously or too literally.

22 WEDNESDAY
Moon Age Day 6 Moon Sign Libra

In general, daily life might seem to take on a fairly routine quality, so if you want any excitement you will probably have to arrange it for yourself. Do something different and unexpected, if only to keep others guessing for a while. The evening has good social potential, but, once again, it's up to you.

23 THURSDAY
Moon Age Day 7 Moon Sign Libra

If you are on holiday at the moment, you have clearly chosen a good time to take a break. Even if this is not the case, you can choose to do something different and interesting on this high-summer Thursday. Don't settle for pointless routines, but instead ring the changes whenever you get the chance.

24 FRIDAY
Moon Age Day 8 Moon Sign Libra

There are some important peaks to be reached before the working week comes to a close. You show yourself to be very capable and able to make the right decisions. If you are between jobs at the moment, you could do much worse that to conduct a search today. Something could be in the offing.

25 SATURDAY   *Moon Age Day 9 Moon Sign Scorpio*

Meetings with others ought to be rather pleasurable and your mind easily turns towards ways and means of having fun. You are humorous, inclined to play practical jokes on others and will be very good company to have around. It looks as though you will also be happy to bring newcomers into your social fold.

26 SUNDAY   *Moon Age Day 10 Moon Sign Scorpio*

You are now inclined to have periods of sudden magnetic attraction in affairs of the heart, which could just turn out to be slightly embarrassing if you find yourself receiving offers you didn't expect. Make your true feelings clear from the start in any contact with others or you may also inspire unnecessary jealousy.

27 MONDAY   *Moon Age Day 11 Moon Sign Sagittarius*

Get an early start today with all-important projects. If you are going to be away from work later, do what you can today to set the seal on specific actions. You won't be inclined to leave anything to chance and this also includes important details relating to future travel.

28 TUESDAY   *Moon Age Day 12 Moon Sign Sagittarius*

This would be another very good day on which to follow your own incentives and ideas. Others will almost naturally follow your lead and although there are moments when you tend to be very reflective, you have what it takes to make most of the social arrangements and to make sure everyone is comfortable.

29 WEDNESDAY   *Moon Age Day 13 Moon Sign Capricorn*

There seems to be a greater willingness to take the lead in romantic matters and although the middle of a working week might seem to be a fairly unlikely time to sweep someone off their feet, you do have that ability. You won't have much time for petty rules or officious people under present planetary trends.

30 THURSDAY   *Moon Age Day 14 Moon Sign Capricorn*

The forces of change are well in place and life should be far from predictable or boring. This suits you down to the ground and you move forward on all fronts with great enthusiasm and a good deal of energy. Not everyone can keep up with your lightning quick thought processes, so be prepared to explain yourself.

31 FRIDAY   *Moon Age Day 15 Moon Sign Aquarius*

Anything to do with travel will certainly make life more interesting, and the lunar high also offers incentives you were not expecting. Turning even difficult situations to your advantage should be quite easy and you are filled with enthusiasm for projects that seem custom-made to keep you happy.

August
2015

1 SATURDAY
Moon Age Day 16 Moon Sign Aquarius

Grasp every new opportunity with both hands and don't squander the positive trends that stand around you now. Whether at work or at play, you are delightful to have around and can make new friends very easily at this time. When it comes to getting on with strangers you are in a really good position today.

2 SUNDAY
Moon Age Day 17 Moon Sign Pisces

Planetary trends show that social and co-operative ventures ought to be working out very well for you at the moment. Although there may be an issue to resolve early in the day, it shouldn't be very long before you are working to the best of your ability and solving a few other problems on the way.

3 MONDAY
Moon Age Day 18 Moon Sign Pisces

A significant lift to your spirits comes along today and there should be some strong social highlights to be enjoyed. An arrangement that is likely to be made by friends might lead to some really interesting interludes, though it is possible that some of these won't actually arrive until later in the week.

4 TUESDAY
Moon Age Day 19 Moon Sign Aries

Don't become over idealistic about a romantic issue. It is possible that you are not seeing things quite as clearly now as you usually do and some impartial advice from a friend could be in order. Make sure your expectations of life are fairly realistic around this time.

5 WEDNESDAY
Moon Age Day 20 Moon Sign Aries

Relationships could prove to be a little troublesome today. In your mind the fault is not yours, but you are reasonable by nature and will come to accept that it takes two to tango. Don't be too quick to make a judgement about a friend who is behaving rather strangely. You might not know all the circumstances.

6 THURSDAY
Moon Age Day 21 Moon Sign Aries

A very short period of greater introspection and evaluation is now around and you will be quite happy to accept that you cannot always be noisy and active. You want to look at things closely and won't be so keen to push ahead with plans until you are certain in your own mind that they are going to work out well.

7 FRIDAY
Moon Age Day 22 Moon Sign Taurus

Things change quickly and it looks as though you are going to be especially assertive and somewhat determined at the moment, which could come as a surprise to your nearest and dearest. Aquarius is usually as pleasant as the day is long, so those who know you best are naturally unsettled on those rare occasions when you are pushy.

8 SATURDAY
Moon Age Day 23 Moon Sign Taurus

Social matters tend to be helpfully highlighted and can lead you to a more progressive phase that is gradually likely to take over. There should be less internal confusion now and this diminishes even more over the next few days. Try to co-operate at work, because to do so can be a definite boon.

9 SUNDAY
Moon Age Day 24 Moon Sign Gemini

Loved ones could prove rather difficult to understand today and a little extra effort on your part is clearly necessary. You might have to put the brake on some social activities for the moment or at least reorganise things in some way. If you are at work, you could make progress without even realising it.

10 MONDAY   *Moon Age Day 25 Moon Sign Gemini*

You now have a great deal of energy that is available to put into whatever takes your fancy. Although there may not be anything particularly important happening at present, you are in a good position to enjoy yourself and also to bring a good deal of happiness into the lives of the people with whom you make contact.

11 TUESDAY   *Moon Age Day 26 Moon Sign Cancer*

Your mind is sharp, making this an especially good day for study or detailed work of any sort. You will be able to come to terms with issues that confused you in the past and won't be at all lazy. Social trends continue to look good and some of the best possibilities come about as a result of a prospective journey.

12 WEDNESDAY   *Moon Age Day 27 Moon Sign Cancer*

You will be feeling very positive about yourself for most of today and can make the best of impressions on the world at large. This is a time to enjoy yourself and there won't be too much time for deep thinking. The future seems to be an unwritten book, which is fine for the moment.

13 THURSDAY   *Moon Age Day 28 Moon Sign Leo*

With the lunar low starting today you could become somewhat disillusioned, though once you realise this you will accept that this is a temporary matter. Stick to routines. These will suit you for the next couple of days and they offer a sense of security.

14 FRIDAY   *Moon Age Day 29 Moon Sign Leo*

Avoid making too many decisions again today and simply go with the flow. There are people around who can even make the period of the lunar low a distinct joy, but you have to give them the benefit of the doubt. Ask for something you want today, because someone close to you is in a generous mood.

15 SATURDAY   *Moon Age Day 0 Moon Sign Leo*

Keep your eyes and ears open now for new information related to personal projects. Today could be something of a mixed bag, because you won't be frightened to look at all aspects of your life, though at the same time you show a great desire to simply have fun. There are plenty of people around who would be willing to join in.

16 SUNDAY   *Moon Age Day 1 Moon Sign Virgo*

You may choose today to assess the progress you have been making in your life generally. Although this will be a busy sort of day, there are moments to think again about specific events and to put right those situations that didn't turn out quite the way you may have expected. You should be very optimistic just now.

17 MONDAY   *Moon Age Day 2 Moon Sign Virgo*

You are likely to be getting the best from both career and personal matters now. Don't worry too much about details, most of which can be sorted out easily. If you feel tired later in the day, be prepared to take a rest and don't push yourself into situations that seem a terrible waste of time.

18 TUESDAY   *Moon Age Day 3 Moon Sign Libra*

It's time for some light relief, even though you may be almost entirely committed to your working life today. The practical joker within you is on display and most people will be happy to go along with your off-the-wall sense of humour. Aquarius is out for fun and this fact extends to your family life, too.

19 WEDNESDAY   *Moon Age Day 4 Moon Sign Libra*

Professional developments may now be going just a little off course, especially if you are over-committed in some way. Try to plan ahead, particularly if you are thinking of making any changes at home. A journey might suit you during the midweek period. If you haven't already arranged it, why not do so this evening?

20 THURSDAY
Moon Age Day 5 Moon Sign Libra

Investing a great deal of confidence in others will occasionally lead to disappointments today. However, that's the way you are and getting your fingers burnt now and again will not change your basic nature – thank goodness. When problems do come along you will deal with them cheerfully.

21 FRIDAY
Moon Age Day 6 Moon Sign Scorpio

There are positive signs where money is concerned. Although you might have to rein in your spending somewhat right now, this fact stands as evidence that you are looking at financial matters more closely. By as early as tomorrow you should find your position generally more secure.

22 SATURDAY
Moon Age Day 7 Moon Sign Scorpio

Getting out and about would work wonders as far as your general attitude is concerned today. Certainly you should avoid being cooped up in the same place for hours on end. Fresh fields and pastures new beckon. Aquarius is definitely in the mood for fun and everyone else will be obliged to join in.

23 SUNDAY
Moon Age Day 8 Moon Sign Sagittarius

You show a strong desire to get your ideas across to others today and a few frustrations could follow if you find that you have some difficulty doing so. Specific people seem to trivialise situations that are very important to you, a fact that may prove quite annoying unless you exercise self-discipline.

24 MONDAY
Moon Age Day 9 Moon Sign Sagittarius

Even casual talks with others could prove enlightening during the present period. This is likely to be especially true at work, with the possibility of promotion coming along for some Aquarians at this time. Keep your most entertaining side hidden until the evening, but then take every opportunity to involve yourself in the happy times on offer.

25 TUESDAY *Moon Age Day 10 Moon Sign Sagittarius*

Much of the fulfilment you experience today lies in private and domestic matters. You won't be able to remove yourself from the real world altogether, even though this is what you might feel like doing at times. This could be a response to a very active period you may have experienced since the weekend.

26 WEDNESDAY *Moon Age Day 11 Moon Sign Capricorn*

It could appear that others are making too much of issues you don't really think are important. Try to stretch your imagination and to see things from their point of view. Socially speaking, you should keep life as simple as you can, associating freely with just about anyone who comes along and chatting at every opportunity.

27 THURSDAY *Moon Age Day 12 Moon Sign Capricorn*

You may be entering a period of escapism. This isn't all that unusual for Aquarius, but you need to be careful that you are not neglecting important jobs you have already started. All the same, there is nothing wrong with being a dreamer now and again. You might even arrive at some significant realisations.

28 FRIDAY *Moon Age Day 13 Moon Sign Aquarius*

Today is favourable for all sorts of new plans and for consolidating past gains in original ways. You are likely to be as sociable as ever and you show great flair when it comes to organising almost anything. Any negative traits of the last few days are nothing but a distant memory as you push forward on all fronts.

29 SATURDAY *Moon Age Day 14 Moon Sign Aquarius*

Now the brakes are really off. The Moon in particular is in an excellent position to allow you to move forward with greater speed and determination than has been possible for quite some time. It looks as though good fortune is on your side and could bring better financial prospects, as well as new opportunities.

30 SUNDAY
Moon Age Day 15 Moon Sign Pisces

There are great opportunities around now for broadening your horizons in a general sense. Whether or not you choose to actually do anything specific today remains to be seen. Any opportunity to be involved in something different is likely to be grabbed with both hands and you show a positive response to suggestions friends are making.

31 MONDAY
Moon Age Day 16 Moon Sign Pisces

Chances are you will still be ready to tackle any sensible sort of challenge today and need to be in a position to know who is going to be on your team. Confidence to speak boldly in company certainly won't be lacking at this time and in many respects you are more dominant now than for the last few weeks.

1 TUESDAY

Moon Age Day 17 Moon Sign Aries

Today marks the start of a period in which travel is well starred, and this would be an excellent time to widen your personal experience at almost any level. Routines are definitely for the birds, because there is so much around you that seems new and exciting. Whether everyone else will agree remains to be seen.

2 WEDNESDAY

Moon Age Day 18 Moon Sign Aries

You should find certain career matters bearing fruit. Some Aquarians will be opting for a completely new start under present influences and even if you are not one of these you will have it within your power to make positive alterations. Colleagues should be especially helpful and fall over themselves to oblige you.

3 THURSDAY

Moon Age Day 19 Moon Sign Taurus

It is likely that your social life and all co-operative ventures have much to offer today. There is a good chance that you will be dealing with some interesting and even quite stimulating people and you love to surround yourself with intelligent types under present trends. A slight threat could be removed.

4 FRIDAY

Moon Age Day 20 Moon Sign Taurus

Your creative intuition is heightened now and your personal life should prove to be rather more comfortable than might have been the case on occasions in the recent past. Get as much change and diversity into your life as you can. Your tendency towards sacrifice on behalf of others will lead to a warm and happy moment.

5 SATURDAY
Moon Age Day 21 Moon Sign Gemini

You will have less time at the moment for social encounters, but only because you are generally so busy. Keeping up appearances will be important to you, though this tends to be restricted to professional matters. Do try to find at least a little time at either end of the day during when you can mix and mingle.

6 SUNDAY
Moon Age Day 22 Moon Sign Gemini

Your daily life should be inspiring and enjoyable. Conversation is definitely your forte right now and there may be significant input coming in from the direction of friends. It is quite easy to be distracted, but you won't mind about that too much. Even apparently irrelevant matters have their part to play in your life.

7 MONDAY
Moon Age Day 23 Moon Sign Cancer

You need to get as much variety into your life as you can at the beginning of this new working week. This means you will not be confining yourself specifically to practical matters, but you will also need to socialise as much as possible. Better still, find new ways in which to mix business with pleasure.

8 TUESDAY
Moon Age Day 24 Moon Sign Cancer

If you can't get away from obligations today try to find ways in which they can be made enjoyable. Almost anything can carry fun with it, such is the nature of the Aquarian individual. Friends you haven't seen for quite some time are likely to return to your life at any time now.

9 WEDNESDAY
Moon Age Day 25 Moon Sign Cancer

You take great pleasure from your creativity and want everything to look just right at the moment. It appears as though you will be very tidy-minded and won't take at all kindly to people who mess things up. Routines are attractive, but your insistence on them could drive others up the wall.

10 THURSDAY
Moon Age Day 26 Moon Sign Leo

It appears that your get-up-and-go somehow got up and went. The lunar low will sap your energy and can make it difficult to maintain the headway that your present nature is demanding. As a result, you find yourself in something of a dilemma. Instead of worrying about this, learn to laugh at yourself.

11 FRIDAY
Moon Age Day 27 Moon Sign Leo

You still won't be exactly on top form and would be better off allowing others to make the running under present trends. Progress comes in fits and starts – that is, if you notice any at all. None of this really matters because it is temporary, but your frustration is the greatest potential stumbling block.

12 SATURDAY
Moon Age Day 28 Moon Sign Virgo

One of your strengths at the moment is your ability to organise. That's fine as far as it goes, but you could annoy colleagues, friends or family members if you push too hard. For now, be content to get your own life in shape. If that indirectly has a bearing on others, then so much the better.

13 SUNDAY
Moon Age Day 0 Moon Sign Virgo

Teamwork and social matters take up a good deal of your time and you continue to show a very positive face to the world at large. There might be time to address romance and to prove to someone you really care for how important they are to you. For young Aquarians, the light of love may shine for the first time now.

14 MONDAY
Moon Age Day 1 Moon Sign Virgo

Bearing in mind a new thrust towards self-determination that is well marked at present, this could turn out to be a very useful sort of Monday indeed. New activities are likely, as well as a period during which you gain a great deal from simply being around much-loved family members and friends.

15 TUESDAY *Moon Age Day 2 Moon Sign Libra*

This is a day during which you should definitely confide your feelings to loved ones. In particular, you could see this as being a time for explaining your ideas and motivations to your partner. You show yourself to be warm, understanding and well able to heal any minor breach that has existed.

16 WEDNESDAY *Moon Age Day 3 Moon Sign Libra*

All of a sudden you could find yourself subject to some moodiness and show a tendency to fall out with people about the most inconsequential matters. It would be a shame to spoil the party just for the sake of a quick passing trend and you can avoid doing so by counting to ten before you say something you might regret later.

17 THURSDAY *Moon Age Day 4 Moon Sign Scorpio*

It's great to have pleasant people around you and that is what seems to be happening right now. This could turn out to be a great time for Aquarians who have decided to take a holiday. Even if you are stuck in your usual rut, you can find ways to ring the changes enough to feel quite content with your lot.

18 FRIDAY ☿ *Moon Age Day 5 Moon Sign Scorpio*

It looks as there will be slight restrictions placed upon your movements today, no matter how much you wish otherwise. Even so, you manage to get through or round these quite easily. You are especially good in conversation at present, and although talking to others is never a problem to you, right now you are positively eloquent.

19 SATURDAY ☿ *Moon Age Day 6 Moon Sign Scorpio*

Interesting gatherings are likely to bring out the best in you and will allow you to make good headway in practical as well as strictly social matters. Mixing business with pleasure is not out of the question at the moment and you appear to have what it takes to push the bounds of the possible even more than usual.

20 SUNDAY ☿ *Moon Age Day 7 Moon Sign Sagittarius*

It's one thing assuming that you are right about something, but quite different to push the issue to such an extent that you fall out with someone. Although you continue to be attentive and kind, you are also rather too emphatic for your own good right now. Just bear in mind that there is always an alternative point of view.

21 MONDAY ☿ *Moon Age Day 8 Moon Sign Sagittarius*

What works best this week is to surround yourself with the right sort of people on each specific occasion. At work you need to be amongst the go-getters and pacesetters, whilst in a social sense you are best off with more compliant and easy-going sorts. All you really need in your personal life is that special someone.

22 TUESDAY ☿ *Moon Age Day 9 Moon Sign Capricorn*

It seems as though your personal and domestic life now takes centre stage and you will probably be finding more time to get on side with family members who could have been rather distant of late. You could also be taking a short journey to see someone who you care for deeply but whom you definitely don't see every day.

23 WEDNESDAY ☿ *Moon Age Day 10 Moon Sign Capricorn*

Love issues could turn out to be far too dramatic and emotional for your liking. This isn't coming from your direction, but you are subject to it all the same. Some Aquarians will therefore be trying to keep lovers at arm's length for a while, or else choosing to mix with those who are friends rather than intimates.

24 THURSDAY *Moon Age Day 11 Moon Sign Aquarius*

The Moon enters Aquarius and brings one of the most potentially powerful times of the month. Now you are definitely on a roll and will not be inclined to stop from morning until night. You are so determined to get ahead that it is very unlikely anyone would think of questioning your motives or actions.

25 FRIDAY ☿ *Moon Age Day 12 Moon Sign Aquarius*

There could be some quite important people around today and you are in just the right frame of mind to make the most out of your association with them. There is more than a little good luck about and plenty of opportunity to push new incentives. Even romance looks sparkling and interesting.

26 SATURDAY ☿ *Moon Age Day 13 Moon Sign Pisces*

You now seem to be very much tuned in to the needs of your partner or significant other. There is less emotional tension around for some of you and a more relaxed atmosphere that proves to be both happy and fulfilling. Whereas it might have appeared that everything you did before was wrong to your lover, now you are flavour of the month.

27 SUNDAY ☿ *Moon Age Day 14 Moon Sign Pisces*

You could hardly choose a better than this to discuss something important. Your approach is casual but attentive and you are unlikely to fall out with anyone. Such is your present charm that you could easily get on side with someone who is usually about as prickly as a cactus, so take advantage of these trends.

28 MONDAY ☿ *Moon Age Day 15 Moon Sign Aries*

Where new professional developments are concerned it looks as though you have your finger on the pulse and you won't have many problems keeping up with new incentives and possibilities. Today would also be good for a shopping spree, especially if you combine it with an outing with friends and maybe a meal thrown in.

29 TUESDAY ☿ *Moon Age Day 16 Moon Sign Aries*

You show keen judgement at work and a strong desire to have things right at home ahead of the upcoming colder days. Maybe you are opting for a decorating spree or replacing certain furnishings. Whatever you decide to buy, it's important to make sure you get a bargain and that you don't lock yourself into very long financial deals.

30 WEDNESDAY ☿   *Moon Age Day 17 Moon Sign Taurus*

You enjoy the company of many different sorts of people out here in the middle of the week and won't want to concentrate too much on any one of your friends. You also find ways to incorporate your deeper emotional attachments with those that are far more casual. The truth is that you want to make everyone as happy as possible.

October
2015

1 THURSDAY ☿ Moon Age Day 18 Moon Sign Taurus

Your major new focus is now on leisure and romantic matters. With everything working generally well you should be able to see quite easily how attractive you are to others. There are distinct gains to be made at this time from simply being what you naturally are. Personalities abound, both at work and socially.

2 FRIDAY ☿ Moon Age Day 19 Moon Sign Gemini

This is a favourable time where your finances are concerned. This would be a good time to look at money and to work out how best to plan for the future. At the same time, there is a strong social quality to the day and you don't have any trouble in mixing business with pleasure.

3 SATURDAY ☿ Moon Age Day 20 Moon Sign Gemini

Although part of you is anxious to make progress, there are aspects of your mind that are restricted and far from forward-looking. Take on board the needs of those close to you and, if at all, possible enjoy a family day. Don't get involved in discussions that could so easily lead to arguments.

4 SUNDAY ☿ Moon Age Day 21 Moon Sign Gemini

You should find that any work in progress at the moment is both rewarding and materially satisfying. There are positive signs around movement on most fronts. Be aware that it might sometimes be difficult to understand the motivations of close relatives and a little probing could be necessary.

5 MONDAY ☿ *Moon Age Day 22 Moon Sign Cancer*

There ought to be plenty of ways you can feed your ego at the moment. After all, it isn't the voracious monster that is the case with some zodiac signs. Nevertheless, you need to be preened now and again and to know how important you are to those around you. Fishing for compliments might bring a bigger than expected catch today.

6 TUESDAY ☿ *Moon Age Day 23 Moon Sign Cancer*

If you have wanted to make any sort of fresh starts, or improvements and changes to your home, this is probably the best time to get cracking. Enlist the support of family members and plan what you are going to do. It's really a case of taking the bull by the horns today.

7 WEDNESDAY ☿ *Moon Age Day 24 Moon Sign Leo*

You may have to cut your losses regarding a present project in order to make the very best of what lies in store for later. Arrangements for later should be made today, especially if you are looking forward to an important social gathering of some sort. Your partner might seem out of sorts today.

8 THURSDAY ☿ *Moon Age Day 25 Moon Sign Leo*

Don't expect life to follow a particularly smooth course today. The lunar low is inclined to bring complications and it can prevent you from following through in projects that are presently quite important to you. Although you are quite sporting at the moment, it will be harder to get past the winning post first.

9 FRIDAY ☿ *Moon Age Day 26 Moon Sign Virgo*

This is probably the best day of the month in which to express your love for someone very special indeed. Although you might be committed to work, you are also entering a period in which a sense of personal freedom is especially important. As a result, you need to try to arrange some sort of break later in the day.

10 SATURDAY ☿ *Moon Age Day 27 Moon Sign Virgo*

With a more competitive streak now firmly on display, you will want to push forward on all fronts. This might not be especially easy and you will need to use extra effort to get ahead of some of the small difficulties that surround you. Acting on impulse comes as second nature.

11 SUNDAY ☿ *Moon Age Day 28 Moon Sign Virgo*

You are willing to work hard and to do whatever it takes to get to your chosen destination. Don't get bogged down with details today, but instead stick to the main themes of life. It's the big picture that counts. By the evening, you will probably be quite happy to relax in the bosom of your family.

12 MONDAY *Moon Age Day 29 Moon Sign Libra*

So far this month, you have made fairly good progress in material matters and now comes a time when it seems important to consolidate your efforts. Some ingenuity is obvious and you can be fairly definite in your actions. That might not seem like much, but it's very important to Aquarius.

13 TUESDAY *Moon Age Day 0 Moon Sign Libra*

Check up on financial management today, because it's possible that you haven't been taking as much notice of your bank account as you should have. Don't worry: things are not likely to be as bad as you might first think. It would be fair to say that you are rather more pessimistic than usual.

14 WEDNESDAY *Moon Age Day 1 Moon Sign Scorpio*

A period of significant progress is still evident, particularly with regard to your personal plans. Specialist help is available when you need it the most and you shouldn't have to look far in order to discover your great potential. Popularity is also high, which is always encouraging.

15 THURSDAY   *Moon Age Day 2 Moon Sign Scorpio*

In-depth discussions will probably take place today, but how much they are worth remains to be seen. In the main, you will want to spend at least short periods of time on your own or in the company of those you love and trust. By tomorrow, any temporary negative trends will be out of the way, so be patient.

16 FRIDAY   *Moon Age Day 3 Moon Sign Scorpio*

New information is likely to put you fully in the picture today, which will enable you to make progress in many different areas of your life. However, much of what stands around you is only potential and the outcome depends on own efforts. Fortunately, there are some very supportive trends around right now.

17 SATURDAY   *Moon Age Day 4 Moon Sign Sagittarius*

There are some important things to do today, but few of them will turn out to be quite as simple as you might wish. Still, it is possible to apply a little concentration, just as long as you don't try to tackle too many tasks at the same time. With communication well starred, later in the day you might get a call you have been expecting for a while.

18 SUNDAY   *Moon Age Day 5 Moon Sign Sagittarius*

Today marks a time when you will be busy enough, but there ought to be moments for contemplation and for getting your head round problems that might have been with you for a while. Even casual conversations can offer significant clues about the best way forward in a practical sense. Meanwhile, you could find love to be inviting.

19 MONDAY   *Moon Age Day 6 Moon Sign Capricorn*

Work and career issues tend to keep you on the go now, and there is hardly likely to be enough time to do everything that you would wish. Keep an open mind when it comes to changes that are now on the cards and don't spend too much time worrying about what might happen. Most decisions will be yours to make.

20 TUESDAY
Moon Age Day 7 Moon Sign Capricorn

Along comes a flurry of social invitations and some of these will detract from your ability to concentrate on strictly practical matters when they matter the most. Never mind. It's an interesting period all the same and, being an Aquarian, you need the stimulus that comes from interacting with others.

21 WEDNESDAY
Moon Age Day 8 Moon Sign Capricorn

You have lots to do at the moment, but you might not be feeling all that bright. The Moon is in your solar twelfth house, which more or less demands at least short periods of meditation and thought. Put a few routines on the backburner and try to enjoy a relaxing sort of evening, at least.

22 THURSDAY
Moon Age Day 9 Moon Sign Aquarius

Positive thinking really does pay off well today. The lunar high brings much-needed light and energy into your life, so virtually nothing is beyond your capabilities. Something that has been at the back of your mind and that has been troubling you of late can now be addressed and settled.

23 FRIDAY
Moon Age Day 10 Moon Sign Aquarius

An element of serendipity shows itself in your life at the moment. There could well be significant gains, even when you are not particularly trying. The world and his dog are willing to help you towards your objectives and there is no doubt at all that a little cheek goes a very long way.

24 SATURDAY
Moon Age Day 11 Moon Sign Pisces

You will now get more involved in domestic matters than has been possible for a week or so. Your mind turns towards the demands that loved ones make of you and much of your spare time is being used to make others feel more secure. Leave a few moments just for yourself and take some time out to meditate.

25 SUNDAY
Moon Age Day 12 Moon Sign Pisces

There are signs that you are going through a fairly stable period where money matters are concerned, so you should be able to deal with financial matters in a positive way. The real prospects for gain seem to be at work and you have all it takes to make a good impression. That might not be much use if you are not a weekend worker.

26 MONDAY
Moon Age Day 13 Moon Sign Aries

Your powers of persuasion are well starred at the moment, so you should have very little difficulty in getting others to follow your lead. This can be especially useful at work, where you are probably in the running for advancement of some sort. The world tends to be the way you make it right now, so think big.

27 TUESDAY
Moon Age Day 14 Moon Sign Aries

Things remain good for you in a social sense now and getting on with people who were difficult a few days ago should be quite easy. Routines could be tiresome, which is exactly why you tend to ignore them if you can. You are on top form artistically and this could be a good time for planning changes at home.

28 WEDNESDAY
Moon Age Day 15 Moon Sign Taurus

There is one specific piece of advice that really matters today: get organised. You really do need to be on the ball and to prove to everyone around you that you know what you are doing and that you have a plan. Once people see that you are not simply bluffing your way through situations, co-operation is assured.

29 THURSDAY
Moon Age Day 16 Moon Sign Taurus

It won't always be easy today to see a point of view that you just don't understand, but it's only a matter of time before explanations are available. It is probable that there are some events taking place right now to which you cannot be a party for the moment. Try to curb your natural curiosity a little.

30 FRIDAY
Moon Age Day 17 Moon Sign Gemini

Intimate relationships bring promising moments and should help the working week to end in a very favourable way. You have what it takes to win hearts, so if there is someone around you have been wishing to sweep off their feet it seems as though this would be a good time to give it a go.

31 SATURDAY
Moon Age Day 18 Moon Sign Gemini

The prospect of new friendships on the horizon is welcome at a time when present attachments might be in doubt. Don't be too worried if you can't get family members to follow your instructions today. Leave them to their own devices and get on with what is important to you now.

November

2015

1 SUNDAY
Moon Age Day 19 Moon Sign Cancer

You need to keep things varied today. The more change and diversity you get into your life, the better you are going to enjoy what this Sunday has to offer. Leave all serious issues until another day and show how spontaneous you can be. You can also gain by simply being in the right place at the best time.

2 MONDAY
Moon Age Day 20 Moon Sign Cancer

You might be slightly better off from a financial point of view than you had been expecting. It could be that you have miscalculated or maybe you have simply been working that much harder of late. In business, this could turn out to be a good time for important decisions that have been delayed.

3 TUESDAY
Moon Age Day 21 Moon Sign Leo

This is a time best used as a rest period between more active interludes. If you insist on knocking your head against a brick wall, all that results is a headache. Rather than struggling on when you know the trends are not good, take some time out to look and listen. The exercise is well worthwhile.

4 WEDNESDAY
Moon Age Day 22 Moon Sign Leo

Another slightly quieter day during which you continue to take stock. It might seem that the world is not an especially friendly place, but that is only because you are more inclined than usual to look on the black side. At least one person proves how concerned he or she is about you.

5 THURSDAY
Moon Age Day 23 Moon Sign Leo

You will probably desire a little privacy at the moment, but this is not a situation that is likely to last very long. On the contrary, by tomorrow you will be right on the ball, so it would be sensible to get yourself ready for what lies ahead. Friends appear to be extra sensitive today.

6 FRIDAY
Moon Age Day 24 Moon Sign Virgo

There is still a busy feel to life, so much so that paying the attention you should to others may now be quite difficult. Keep as focused as possible, because there are many potential distractions and one or two could lead you in entirely the wrong direction. Don't be frightened of your own success if it materialises.

7 SATURDAY
Moon Age Day 25 Moon Sign Virgo

Getting your own way should not be all that difficult. Rather than simply settling for what seems like a compromise, push forward and go for gold. Routines can be a bit of a drag and there is every reason to believe you will be ringing the changes in both your working life and at home.

8 SUNDAY
Moon Age Day 26 Moon Sign Libra

With great willpower and self-confidence, you are now inclined to take life by the scruff of the neck and to shake it into the shape you wish. This might mean having to be slightly less considerate of the needs of others, but even Aquarius has to be just a little selfish once in a while.

9 MONDAY
Moon Age Day 27 Moon Sign Libra

Practical matters should progress well at the beginning of this week and you are pretty much committed to your work. If you are engaged in full-time education, you need to study harder than ever now. It isn't so much what you know that counts, but rather the way you put it across.

10 TUESDAY
Moon Age Day 28 Moon Sign Libra

You have a natural instinct for analysing all situations today and tend to reach some quite radical conclusions as a result. Not everyone is what they appear to be, something you realise now with startling clarity. Keep your considered opinions to yourself for just a day or two longer.

11 WEDNESDAY
Moon Age Day 29 Moon Sign Scorpio

You will do your very best to arrive at decisions that suit the greatest number of people today, but you have to bear in mind that you can rarely (if ever) please everyone. In the main, you are in harmony with your surroundings and won't be too anxious to upset any applecart, be it social or personal.

12 THURSDAY
Moon Age Day 0 Moon Sign Scorpio

In some circles, a few people will consider your present style to be too impulsive, but they are almost certain to be attracted to you all the same. A positive attitude on your part, coupled with an understanding of necessary actions, will certainly pay dividends. You won't be keen to stand in any queue at the moment.

13 FRIDAY
Moon Age Day 1 Moon Sign Sagittarius

Avoid being too impulsive when you know that a more measured approach would please others more. You are always good at weighing up those around you and this ability is stronger than ever now. Use it to your advantage, even if this means a little manipulation on your part.

14 SATURDAY
Moon Age Day 2 Moon Sign Sagittarius

The planetary emphasis is now on finances and the sense of personal security that seems to be so important to you. At the same time, you are showing a very original streak in your social life and should be mixing with individuals who have not formed a part of your immediate circle before.

15 SUNDAY   *Moon Age Day 3 Moon Sign Sagittarius*

Now you are intent on helping others at a practical level. Little things you do for them have big consequences later on and what you excel at the most is inspiring confidence. This is a Sunday that gets you noticed by those around you and during which you don't tend to procrastinate at all.

16 MONDAY   *Moon Age Day 4 Moon Sign Capricorn*

There could be just a little luck in the financial sphere around this time and you need to be on the ball when it comes to any sort of deal that is in the offing. Look out for the odd practical mishap that could result from you being a little clumsier than usual.

17 TUESDAY   *Moon Age Day 5 Moon Sign Capricorn*

Take a little trip and make some changes to the routines of your life, if you can. It would be all too easy to become bored with things at the moment and in order to avoid this happening you may have to put in a little extra effort. You presently show great consideration for family members.

18 WEDNESDAY   *Moon Age Day 6 Moon Sign Aquarius*

This should turn out to be a day that is especially fulfilling. Whatever you decide to do is accomplished with little effort and you should keep a smile on your face for most of the time. Fresh starts are indicated and these are just as likely in your home life as they are at work.

19 THURSDAY   *Moon Age Day 7 Moon Sign Aquarius*

Today is a high spot and a time when Lady Luck is with you. Thoughts of comfort and security are out of the window, because you are more than willing to take a chance and to push things further than usual. Personal attachments are favoured today.

20 FRIDAY
Moon Age Day 8 Moon Sign Pisces

You remain basically optimistic and committed to the future, though there could be the odd setback today. You will need to keep your wits about you if you don't want to start again at the beginning with some specific projects. It may be best to settle for a fairly steady day – but that might be too much to expect.

21 SATURDAY
Moon Age Day 9 Moon Sign Pisces

You are likely to be out and about more than ever today and the weekend offers much to those Aquarians who are genuinely willing to put themselves out. There isn't any use in waiting around for anyone else to make the arrangements. Although you will have to work hard to get others involved, the effort will be more than worthwhile.

22 SUNDAY
Moon Age Day 10 Moon Sign Aries

Learning new things can be a great deal of fun this Sunday and you launch yourself into projects with a great deal of enthusiasm. Certain people could prove to be difficult, so you will have to show great diplomacy if you are to avoid getting into some sort of disagreement or even a downright row.

23 MONDAY
Moon Age Day 11 Moon Sign Aries

Communication with others is enlivening and even exciting at the start of this new working week. You tend to be acting on impulse for much of the time, but this is so much a part of your basic nature that it isn't any sort of problem. Listen to the ideas of a colleague because they could suit you, too.

24 TUESDAY
Moon Age Day 12 Moon Sign Taurus

It is likely that you will be somewhat argumentative today and you need to curb this tendency if you want to avoid falling out with someone who is in a position to do you a great deal of good. Count to ten before you react and keep your cool, even when you are faced with people you see as being deliberately stupid.

25 WEDNESDAY *Moon Age Day 13 Moon Sign Taurus*

This should prove to be one of the better days of the month during which to enjoy friendship and the simple things of life. If you feel a bit lacklustre, a temporary change of scene could do the trick. When a particular task gets boring or frustrating, put it aside for a while.

26 THURSDAY *Moon Age Day 14 Moon Sign Gemini*

Family and domestic situations are likely to prevail today. Get together with your loved ones and make some plans for the future. It is likely that one of your chief concerns will be Christmas, which is only a month away. When it comes to domestic chores, do your best to be inventive and to change the order in which you do things.

27 FRIDAY *Moon Age Day 15 Moon Sign Gemini*

Look towards a relaxing and interesting sort of day, but also a time during which you will have to think deeply about an issue that has been on your mind for a while. You are quite chilled out at present, so you can deal with situations better and can find answers that have eluded you for a few weeks or even months.

28 SATURDAY *Moon Age Day 16 Moon Sign Cancer*

Beware of situations that could take you by surprise. Most of these are likely to be positive in nature and it appears that you are about to reap the benefits of efforts you have put in previously. The warmest and most endearing qualities of your nature are on display this weekend.

29 SUNDAY *Moon Age Day 17 Moon Sign Cancer*

You need to widen your horizons whenever you can. Don't just look at the possible, but also stretch yourself whenever you can. The tendency to feel bored by life is hovering around and you need to do everything you can to counteract this trend. Seek out interesting people and new situations.

30 MONDAY *Moon Age Day 18 Moon Sign Cancer*

Take every possible opportunity to get away from the ordinary in life. Winter is here and things can start to look very grey and uninspiring unless you put in that extra bit of effort. Aquarius has the power to lift its own spirits and those of everyone with whom it comes into contact.

December
2015

1 TUESDAY
Moon Age Day 19 Moon Sign Leo

You must guard against negative thinking. It would be a mistake to let any vital information pass you by, so it is important to keep looking and listening. Someone is in a very good position to offer you invaluable assistance, but that isn't much use if you fail to notice the fact.

2 WEDNESDAY
Moon Age Day 20 Moon Sign Leo

Perhaps it is now time to let go of the reins for a few hours and to allow others to do the driving. The lunar low is inclined to make you feel less positive and also saps your strength significantly. It isn't that anything specific is likely to go wrong, merely that you are not quite as positive as you have been of late.

3 THURSDAY
Moon Age Day 21 Moon Sign Virgo

The potential for success exists in all matters to do with communication. You know what to say and have the knowing knack of getting others to do your bidding. Using a mixture of psychology and simple logic, you are even able to wind superiors and colleagues around your little finger.

4 FRIDAY
Moon Age Day 22 Moon Sign Virgo

You could do with a slightly firmer approach to family or domestic matters, maybe because those around you are allowing things to drift. Taking the initiative comes as second nature under present planetary trends, even if that means you rub someone up the wrong way as a result.

149

5 SATURDAY   *Moon Age Day 23 Moon Sign Libra*

News that is significant and even heart-warming seems to be coming your way at any time now. There is a practical element to everything you do, but it is quite feasible to mix business with pleasure. Romance shines out in the evening and social trends are gradually looking better.

6 SUNDAY   *Moon Age Day 24 Moon Sign Libra*

Your natural generosity will attract a good deal of attention, but you need to keep your eye on expenditure. It's all very well splashing money about, but you are going to need quite a lot before this month is out. Make sure the assistance you give is in kind and not in cash.

7 MONDAY   *Moon Age Day 25 Moon Sign Libra*

There is likely to be a restlessness about you at the start of this working week and you certainly will not take kindly to others telling you what you should be doing. You know your own routines best and will be anxious to follow your own ideas, especially when it comes to work.

8 TUESDAY   *Moon Age Day 26 Moon Sign Scorpio*

Persuasive and communicative, you must guard against negative thinking, but you do have a great set of incentives and should find it child's play to get others to follow your lead. As the day goes on, you discover more and more that pleases you, and tend to be quite attractive to those around you.

9 WEDNESDAY   *Moon Age Day 27 Moon Sign Scorpio*

Though the obligations you feel to others might be slightly frustrating today, you do need to bear them in mind. They say that no person is an island, and this is particularly true in your case at the moment. If you alienate yourself from those who have it in their power to help you, the results could be tiresome.

10 THURSDAY   *Moon Age Day 28 Moon Sign Sagittarius*

Although personal relationships might be rather downbeat for now, you need to take your joys where you can find them. Today that means friendship and the support that particular individuals are offering. In a practical sense, it would be best not to take anything for granted, especially at work.

11 FRIDAY   *Moon Age Day 0 Moon Sign Sagittarius*

Friday should bring a period of swifter progress. If you put on a spurt, you can steal a march on someone who has been beating you to the punch, though without upsetting him or her too much. What matters at present is convincing yourself that you are as capable as you believe yourself to be when you are at your most confident.

12 SATURDAY   *Moon Age Day 1 Moon Sign Sagittarius*

You might be in the mood for Christmas shopping today, but save your money for another day to avoid making spur-of-the-moment purchases. Friends should be especially helpful and can offer you some timely advice. Make certain you listen carefully to what they are saying.

13 SUNDAY   *Moon Age Day 2 Moon Sign Capricorn*

You seem as though you are very duty-bound on this Sunday. It could be that family members are relying on you heavily and you won't want to let them down. Avoid rows by explaining yourself fully and allow younger family members to have more responsibility for their own lives.

14 MONDAY   *Moon Age Day 3 Moon Sign Capricorn*

Someone higher up the career ladder than you are can steer you in the right direction, if you are only willing to listen to what he or she says. Reliance on friends is strong and new pals could be formed around this period. At least part of your mind is now likely to be focused on Christmas.

15 TUESDAY   *Moon Age Day 4 Moon Sign Aquarius*

The lunar high for December gives you everything you need to get ahead in a practical sense. The only slight problem could be getting others to maintain the pace you are setting. Active and enterprising, you give yourself fully to all new projects and show a positive response to work-related matters.

16 WEDNESDAY   *Moon Age Day 5 Moon Sign Aquarius*

It hasn't been like Aquarius to tempt fate recently, but that is exactly what you will be doing today. You are willing to take almost any sort of chance, because you know your own capabilities – and in any case, the excitement of the situation is what captures your imagination. Money matters should be easier to negotiate.

17 THURSDAY   *Moon Age Day 6 Moon Sign Pisces*

Emotional ties prove to be very powerful and this is a time when personal attachments mean the most. You are still active and enterprising, so will be looking for excitement. However, you are likely to be sharing adventures with your partner or family members you look upon with great affection.

18 FRIDAY   *Moon Age Day 7 Moon Sign Pisces*

You are in the mood for fun today, rather than being too tied down with the realities of work, and there should be many people around who are willing to join you. Stay away from negative people or individuals who are backbiting and cruel. The closer you are to the people you are dealing with personally, the better you will feel.

19 SATURDAY   *Moon Age Day 8 Moon Sign Aries*

Take some time out to think things through. Your mind is presently uncluttered with irrelevant details and you see clearly through to the heart of most situations. Reassure those with whom you live that you have been thinking about the festive season and that many of the necessary details are sorted.

20 SUNDAY
Moon Age Day 9 Moon Sign Aries

Some fairly interesting news is likely to come along and this allows you to address your own needs and wishes. Getting on with the task in hand is paramount, but there are so many distractions coming in from all quarters that this could be difficult. You definitely have one eye on the demands of Christmas.

21 MONDAY
Moon Age Day 10 Moon Sign Aries

Stronger than normal personal ego is likely under present trends. You might be taking on rather too much just now and a little fresh air would do you good. You need some space to think things through and to put the brakes on your present tendency to lord it slightly over others. This isn't usual for Aquarius.

22 TUESDAY
Moon Age Day 11 Moon Sign Taurus

Your powers of attraction are strong right now and that can prove to be very useful. The bearing you have on the thinking processes of those around you may be quite surprising and could lead you to taking the odd risk when dealing with your partner or sweetheart. You should throw caution to the wind in at least one matter.

23 WEDNESDAY
Moon Age Day 12 Moon Sign Taurus

This would be a good day for asking questions and for gathering new information about life and the part you play in it. Be careful with last-minute shopping. You could be fooled into thinking that you are getting a bargain, when you know in your heart that you are being conned.

24 THURSDAY
Moon Age Day 13 Moon Sign Gemini

Things ought to be working out reasonably well for you, particularly if you are working on Christmas Eve. Getting things to slot into place should be easy enough and you do show a great deal of respect for those with whom you work. Things at home are likely to be frenetic and none too comfortable on occasion.

25 FRIDAY
Moon Age Day 14   Moon Sign Gemini

You have a good knack for dealing with different sorts of people on this Christmas Day and show great adaptability. There is a slight restlessness around you and that means you will be happier to be on the move, rather than sitting in a chair and toasting your toes in front of the fire. Stay away from party games, because they will bore you now.

26 SATURDAY
Moon Age Day 15   Moon Sign Cancer

You need to tie up loose ends today and to get yourself ready for the end of the year bash. Resolutions are likely to come into your mind already, but you need to keep these as realistic as possible. Don't be too keen to alter anything today, but rather keep on your planning head.

27 SUNDAY
Moon Age Day 16   Moon Sign Cancer

You might receive a financial boost that could help you follow your own plans once the New Year gets underway. At the moment, this might represent little more than a promise, but it proves to be good news all the same. What it means beyond anything else is that those in positions of authority have confidence in you.

28 MONDAY
Moon Age Day 17   Moon Sign Leo

Energy levels are like to be down today, thanks to the lunar low. This really is the sort of day when you ought to be thinking about simple pleasures and good company. You are on the go for most of the time, so there is nothing wrong with taking a break.

29 TUESDAY
Moon Age Day 18   Moon Sign Leo

The Moon is still in Leo and that means the lunar low continues to have a bearing on your attitudes and actions. As New Year approaches, you will be right back on form, but for the moment you are more likely to be watching and waiting. Anything with an artistic association is likely to please you today.

30 WEDNESDAY   *Moon Age Day 19 Moon Sign Virgo*

This is a day when you should be prepared to let everyone know exactly who you are. Once you have decided on a particular course of action, you are inclined to stick with it to the bitter end. New Year resolutions are still on your mind and you will be putting some of them into action early.

31 THURSDAY   *Moon Age Day 20 Moon Sign Virgo*

Things are speeding up. There are some great things happening on the social horizon and you ought to be in a good position to gain from them today. Any slight frustration that the holidays are preventing you from getting ahead in more practical ways will soon be forgotten once you are fully into the New Year celebrations.

RISING SIGNS FOR AQUARIUS

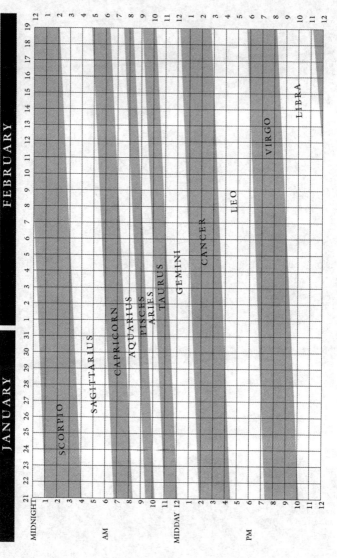

THE ZODIAC, PLANETS AND CORRESPONDENCES

The Earth revolves around the Sun once every calendar year, so when viewed from Earth the Sun appears in a different part of the sky as the year progresses. In astrology, these parts of the sky are divided into the signs of the zodiac and this means that the signs are organised in a circle. The circle begins with Aries and ends with Pisces.

Taking the zodiac sign as a starting point, astrologers then work with all the positions of planets, stars and many other factors to calculate horoscopes and birth charts and tell us what the stars have in store for us.

The table below shows the planets and Elements for each of the signs of the zodiac. Each sign belongs to one of the four Elements: Fire, Air, Earth or Water. Fire signs are creative and enthusiastic; Air signs are mentally active and thoughtful; Earth signs are constructive and practical; Water signs are emotional and have strong feelings.

It also shows the metals and gemstones associated with, or corresponding with, each sign. The correspondence is made when a metal or stone possesses properties that are held in common with a particular sign of the zodiac.

Finally, the table shows the opposite of each star sign – this is the opposite sign in the astrological circle.

Placed	Sign	Symbol	Element	Planet	Metal	Stone	Opposite
1	Aries	Ram	Fire	Mars	Iron	Bloodstone	Libra
2	Taurus	Bull	Earth	Venus	Copper	Sapphire	Scorpio
3	Gemini	Twins	Air	Mercury	Mercury	Tiger's Eye	Sagittarius
4	Cancer	Crab	Water	Moon	Silver	Pearl	Capricorn
5	Leo	Lion	Fire	Sun	Gold	Ruby	Aquarius
6	Virgo	Maiden	Earth	Mercury	Mercury	Sardonyx	Pisces
7	Libra	Scales	Air	Venus	Copper	Sapphire	Aries
8	Scorpio	Scorpion	Water	Pluto	Plutonium	Jasper	Taurus
9	Sagittarius	Archer	Fire	Jupiter	Tin	Topaz	Gemini
10	Capricorn	Goat	Earth	Saturn	Lead	Black Onyx	Cancer
11	Aquarius	Waterbearer	Air	Uranus	Uranium	Amethyst	Leo
12	Pisces	Fishes	Water	Neptune	Tin	Moonstone	Virgo

Capricorn	23rd Dec – 20th Jan
Aquarius	21st Jan – 19th Feb
Pisces	20th Feb – 20th M
Aries	21st Mar 20th Apr.
Taurus	21st Apr – 21st May
Gemini	22nd May 21st June
Cancer	22nd June 22nd July